The Primary Comprehension Toolkit

Strategy Book 3: Ask Questions

Curiosity is at the heart of teaching and learning. Young kids burst through the door bubbling over with questions. *Why is the sky blue? Where does the sun go at night? What happened to the cowboys?* Questions spur curious minds to investigate. Questions open the doors to understanding the world. We have to mine them with a pickaxe! As young readers read nonfiction and meet new information, they brim with questions. As they try to answer their questions, they discover new information and gain knowledge. Questions spark further research and inquiry. Instead of demanding answers all the time, we need to teach kids to ask thoughtful and insightful questions. If we hope to develop critical thinkers, we must teach our kids to think about and question what they listen to, read, and view. Asking questions enriches the learning experience and leads to deeper understanding. Questioning is the strategy that propels learners on.

Lessons

In the Toolkit, we emphasize reading, writing, and drawing to explore and learn about the world.

In this Strategy Book, the lessons for questioning are:

Strategy Support

firsthand
HEINEMANN
DEDICATED TO TEACHERS™

Copyright 2008 by Stephanie Harvey and Anne Goudvis. All rights reserved.

The authors and publisher wish to thank those who have generously given permission to reprint borrowed materials.

Library of Congress Cataloging-in-Publication Data
CIP data on file with the Library of Congress

Ask Questions
ISBN-13: 978-0-325-02150-8
ISBN-10: 0-325-02150-3

Primary Comprehension Toolkit: Language and Lessons for Active Literacy
ISBN-13: 978-0-325-00997-1
ISBN-10: 0-325-00997-X

Printed in the United States of America on acid-free paper

14 13   ML   5

View and Read to Learn and Wonder

Text Matters

When teaching readers to think about new information and wonder about it, we search for text on a familiar and intriguing topic that is also likely to contain ideas that kids don't already know. It is the fresh information that lends itself to wondering. Questions come quickly on the heels of new facts and concepts. As kids activate background knowledge to better understand new information, they may come to see that they have prior misconceptions, which reading and learning can reverse. As always with primary kids, we make sure to choose text with compelling images, so that they are more apt to pay attention, notice new information, and wonder about it.

Resources&Materials

Lesson Text
TIME For Kids Bigger Picture Edition [Fall 2002] "Spiders!" poster

Classroom Supplies
- *What We Think We Know/What We Learned* Anchor Chart and marker
- Post-its

Student Supplies
- Clipboard with *I Learned/I Wonder* Thinksheet and Post-its or Post-its Thinksheets [See *Strategy Book 3*, pages 67–69, or the DVD-ROM.]
- Student copy of "Spiders" [See *Keep Reading! A Source Book of Short Text*, pages 5–8, or the DVD-ROM.]
- Assorted markers, pencils, and crayons

Use images and words to gain understanding

Goals & Assessment

We want students to:

- use text and images to understand.

- think and wonder about new learning.

- jot down new learning and questions on Post-its and then sort them in two columns: *I Learned* and *I Wonder.*

- understand that misconceptions are normal and that learners revise their thinking after reading and listening to additional information.

Why & What

Background knowledge is the primary determinant of comprehension. Nonfiction reading in particular requires readers to think about what they know in order to understand new information. So we encourage kids to ask questions about new information to make sure they understand it. In this lesson, kids use a thinksheet titled *I Learned/I Wonder* to support understanding as they meet new information while reading. Sometimes young children have limited or inaccurate background knowledge and develop misconceptions. In this lesson, we create a class Anchor Chart titled *What We Think We Know/What We Learned* before we read about the new topic. Then after reading, we go back and notice whether what we thought we knew was accurate and we celebrate how reading changes thinking and clears up prior misconceptions.

How

Connect and Engage

- Engage kids by holding up the book or magazine cover and enthusiastically reading the title aloud.

- Record what kids think they know about the topic on the *What We Think We Know/What We Learned* Anchor Chart.

Model

- Share the two-column *I Learned/I Wonder* Thinksheet. Explain that sometimes when we learn new information, we wonder about it. Invite kids to respond.

- Respond to a photograph. Show how you think and wonder about images to gain understanding.

- Model for kids how to record learning and wondering on Post-its and place them in the appropriate column of the thinksheet.

Guide

- Engage kids in the process by reading aloud and guiding the discussion.

- Have them record what they learn and wonder on Post-its and then put the Post-its in the appropriate column of the thinksheet.

Collaborate

- Invite kids to join with a partner and continue reading the text and looking at the pictures, jotting their new learning and wondering on their thinksheets.

- Move around the room and confer with partners.

Share the Learning

- Invite kids to share their new learning as well as anything they wonder.

- Review the *What We Think We Know/What We Learned* Anchor Chart to discover any new thinking and learning.

Used with permission from *TIME For Kids*.

Lesson Text

The *TIME For Kids* Bigger Picture Edition "Spiders!" is a great poster that is guaranteed to captivate kids. When it comes to learning and wondering, the spiders topic is near the top of the list in terms of creating interest. Most kids just can't get enough of spiders and insects. A large photo of a colorful spider on the cover, a variety of spider photos inside, and a diagram of spider body parts on the back cover get kids to notice and wonder about spiders. There is enough new, surprising information that we are likely to clear up a misconception or two in the process of reading this article.

TEACHING MOVES | **TEACHING LANGUAGE**

Connect and Engage

Engage kids by holding up the book or magazine cover and enthusiastically reading the title aloud.

Wow! Take a look at this picture! What do you think about spiders? What do you wonder about them? What do you think you know about them? A lot of you already have some background knowledge (BK) about spiders. Turn to each other and talk about spiders. *[Kids turn and talk enthusiastically about spiders.]*

Today we are going look at this poster about spiders and view some of the images. Viewing means we look at the pictures, the photographs, and the features to get information. We will also read about spiders to learn more. But before we do that, I want to record some things we *think* we already know about spiders on this chart. *[I point to chart.]*

Record what kids think they know about the topic on the *What We Think We Know/What We Learned* Anchor Chart.

Who wants to share what you think you know about spiders, your background knowledge about spiders? I'll write your ideas on the chart.

Ted: Spiders have eight legs.

Ann: Some spiders have wings.

Jo: All spiders spin webs.

[More kids share ideas and I write them down.]

So many great thoughts about spiders! Now we are going to read and view this very cool spider poster. After we have finished reading, we will come back to our chart and see if we have any new ideas or if we have changed our thinking at all.

What We Think We Know	What We Learned
Spiders have 8 legs.	
Some spiders have wings.	
All spiders spin webs.	
Spiders are hairy.	
Spiders do not have antennas.	
Spiders have 3 body parts.	
Some spiders are poisonous.	

Model

Recently, we have been working on noticing and thinking about new learning and marking a Post-it with an *L* when we learn something new. Today, as I read about spiders and view the pictures, I am going to jot down my new learning on a Post-it. Then I am going to put my Post-it on this *I Learned/I Wonder* Thinksheet in the column that says *I Learned*. The second column says *I Wonder*. Sometimes when we learn new information, we wonder about it. If I wonder something as I read about spiders, I will write what I wonder on a Post-it and then put it in the *I Wonder* column.

Share the two-column *I Learned/I Wonder* Thinksheet. Explain that sometimes when we learn new information, we wonder about it. Invite kids to respond.

OK, first of all, what is the title of this article? *[I point to title.]*

All: "Feed Me."

So what do you think? Why is the article called "Feed Me"? Any ideas? Turn and talk. *[Kids turn and talk. Then I call on someone to share.]* Tanner, why did you think the article is called "Feed Me"?

Tanner: It's about how spiders eat.

Good thinking. Sounds like we are going to learn a lot of different ways that spiders catch their food and eat it. Let's read on:

When a spider is hungry, watch out! Spiders have many amazing ways to trap insects. Some can even catch a fish!

Now that is surprising information. Turn and talk about any new information you learned from what I just read. *[Kids turn and talk.]*

Jenny: Spiders catch fish! I never knew that.

I didn't either, Jenny.

Jeremiah: They trap insects in lots of ways, not just in webs.

So they do, Jeremiah. You used your background knowledge about webs to understand new information. Let's read on and find out more information.

I am going to show you how I learn and wonder about the information. As I look at this page, I am really interested in the photograph of the spider in this bubble. I *wonder* what the bubble is for, so I am going to write that question on a Post-it and put it in the *I Wonder* column. I am also going to draw a picture of a spider in a bubble with a question mark next to it. Then I won't forget my question. *[I hold up the poster and point to the caption.]* Maybe if I read this caption below the photograph, I will find out:

Respond to a photograph. Show how you think and wonder about images to gain understanding.

Spiders go fishing. The water spider floats underwater in a bubble web. It sticks out its legs to fish. Then it pulls in its meal.

Wow! I never knew that. This bubble is a special kind of spider web. It doesn't look like any web I have ever seen. I'm going to mark my Post-it with an *L* and write down what I learned. I have never heard of a bubble web. I thought spiders spin webs out of silk. So interesting.

Model for kids how to record learning and wondering on Post-its and place them in the appropriate column of the thinksheet.

Guide

OK, let's try this together. *[I hand out clipboards with* I Learned/I Wonder *Thinksheets and six Post-its. Then I hold up the poster and point to the image of the spider in the air.]* Let's look at the photograph of the spider that is in the air. I'll read what it says:

> *Spiders jump. The jumping spider spots an insect. It flies through the air. Pounce! It has its dinner.*

If you learned something new in the part I just read or from looking at this photo, jot down and/or draw your new learning. Remember to mark your Post-it with *L. [Kids jot down their new learning.]* Who wants to share?

Marcus: Spiders jump. I never knew that.

That is weird. We don't often think of spiders as jumpers. Good noticing, Marcus. Did anyone wonder anything?

Jake: What does *pounce* mean?

Jordan: It's like a fast jump.

Exactly. The spider surprises the insect by jumping really fast, by pouncing. I'm going to write *some spiders jump* on my Post-it and mark it with *L* for *learn.*

Sherri: It said the spider flies through the air. Do spiders have wings? I wonder.

Such a good question. Did you write it down?

Sherri: No.

Well, write it down. You wouldn't want to forget such an important question. We write down our thinking so we don't forget it.

Do spiders have wings? Hmmm. Let's see if we can find out. The text said spiders fly through the air. I'm going to write your question—*Do spiders have wings?*—because I wonder about it, too. I don't notice any wings in these photos. You can get a lot of information from photos, but we don't have photos of every spider here. I may find the answer as I read on. You never know. If you have anything you wonder, jot it down on a Post-it and put it in the *I Wonder* column of the thinksheet. You can wonder about an image as well as the words. *[I save the* I Learned/I Wonder *chart for use later in the lesson.]*

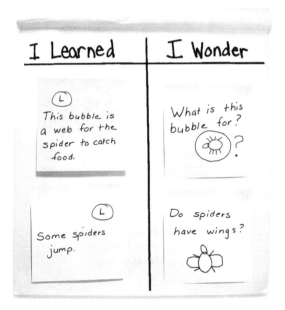

Collaborate

You have done a great job so far. Now it's time for you to work with a partner. I will give each of you a small copy of the poster. Read through it and look carefully at the pictures, noticing and thinking about any new learning you have as well as anything you wonder. Then jot down or draw your thinking on a Post-it and put it in the matching column on the *I Learned/I Wonder* Thinksheet. *[I hand out copies of the poster.]* Remember to think about the pictures and the words. Any questions? OK, have fun!

[I stop by Ali and Whitney.] So how are you two doing?

Ali: We never knew that some spiders work in groups.

Whitney: They weave huge webs together and catch giant prey.

Ali: The webs are as big as trees, like this picture shows.

So you learned that information from the photograph. Good noticing. Did you jot down your new learning?

Whitney: No, we were just talking about it.

That's OK, but it is a good idea to write it down. Why?

Ali: Because it's easier to remember.

Exactly! Such good thinking. So where would you put the Post-it with this information? In the *I Learned* column or in the *I Wonder* column?

Whitney: In the *I Learned* column.

Perfect! Go ahead and jot down that new learning and put the Post-it in the *I Learned* column.

[I check in with Mario and Devon.] What's up with you guys?

Mario: We found something out.

Really, what was that?

Devon: I don't think spiders have wings.

What makes you say that, Devon?

Devon: I found this diagram of a spider on the back page. It shows the body parts, but there are no wings. *[Devon shows the diagram.]*

Exactly. You two are so thoughtful to use the diagram to answer your question. We learn so much by viewing, by looking at the features. I don't see any wings either. Will you please share that information with the class later, during sharing circle? It is so cool when we find out an answer to something we wonder. Be sure to write it down so you won't forget.

Move around the room and confer with partners.

TIP: We encourage kids to write and/or draw what they learn and wonder on Post-its first and then transfer those Post-its to the thinksheet. This scaffolds them to organize their thinking on the thinksheet, so that they will be better prepared to write directly on the thinksheet later on.

Share the Learning

[Kids bring the spider articles along with their thinksheets up and gather together in a sharing circle. They invite one another to share something they learned and something they wonder. As they share, kids hold up their thinksheets and read the Post-its with their new learning or wondering or show a drawing that represents their new learning or wondering. After they share, they ask if there are any questions or comments and they choose one or two classmates who have a question or a comment and respond to them. I invite Mario and Devon to share because I want all of the kids to notice what they inferred from the diagram.]

Devon and Mario found an answer to something they wondered. Would you guys like to share?

Devon: Yes, thank you. We wondered if spiders have wings, just like Sherri did. And then we found this diagram of a spider on the back page.

[Devon holds up the diagram.]

Invite kids to share their new learning as well as anything they wonder.

Mario: We looked at this diagram of the spider parts, but there were no wings. So, we think that spiders do not have wings.

What do the rest of you think? Turn to a partner and talk about it. *[Kids turn and talk.]*

Sherri: I agree with Devon and Mario. I had that question too, but I didn't see the diagram until now.

The diagram really helps to answer that question, doesn't it? It's really important to look closely at the images in photos, diagrams, and illustrations. We can learn so much from viewing. Devon and Mario, great noticing! I agree that spiders do not have wings. That is something we can know for sure now.

You all have done a wonderful job noticing new learning and wondering about it. Let's take a look at the *What We Think We Know/What We Learned* Anchor Chart we created before we started the lesson. I think this diagram that Devon and Mario found can help us. *[I point to the entries on the chart.]*

Spiders have eight legs. We can count them on the diagram. Sure enough. Let's count them together. *[In unison.]* 12345678!!! Eight legs. So we knew that before we even read this article. Here we wrote *Some spiders have wings.* What did Devon and Mario discover?

All: That spiders do not have wings.

Exactly. I think we can change our thinking and cross out *Spiders have wings* and write *Spiders do not have wings* in the *I Learned* column. What about this one? *All spiders spin webs.* Turn to each other and talk: What do you think about that, now that you have read the article? *[Kids turn and talk.]*

Jeremiah: The trapdoor spider builds a hole, not a web.

Great noticing, Jeremiah. We learned that some spiders spin webs, but not all spiders spin webs. Let's cross out *All spiders spin webs* and write that new information in the *What We Learned* column. This is so cool. Before we read this article, we thought all spiders spin webs and now we have learned that some do and some don't. That's what reading is all about: learning new information. What else did you learn?

Samantha: I think spiders have two body parts, not three. Insects have three body parts, but this diagram shows two body parts of the spider.

Good thinking, Samantha. The diagram is really helpful. We can add *Spiders have two body parts* in the *What We Learned* column.

Look, we knew quite a bit of information about spiders before we read the article, but we learned some new information and even changed our thinking after reading, which is so cool. As we read through the article and looked at the photographs, we jotted down our new learning and wondering. We found that reading and viewing pictures give us more information and sometimes change our thinking. That's what education is all about! Great work today, all of you.

Review the *What We Think We Know/What We Learned* Anchor Chart to discover any new thinking and learning.

TIP: As we review what we thought we knew, we discover a few misconceptions. We want our kids to understand that misconceptions are normal and that we need not be embarrassed by them. One of the main reasons we read, listen, and view is to revise our thinking and clear up misconceptions. We want kids to know that the more we read and talk, and the more accurate information we can gather, the more likely we are able to reverse our misconceptions.

What We Think We Know	What We Learned
Spiders have 8 legs.	
~~Some spiders have wings.~~	Spiders do not have wings.
~~All spiders spin webs.~~	Some spiders spin webs.
Spiders are hairy.	
Spiders do not have antennas.	
~~Spiders have 3 body parts.~~	Spiders have 2 body parts.
Some spiders are poisonous.	

Did your students:

- use text and images to understand?

- think and wonder about new learning?

- jot down new learning and questions on Post-its and then sort them in two columns: *I Learned* and *I Wonder*?

- understand that misconceptions are normal and that learners revise their thinking after reading and listening to additional information?

Reflect& Assess

The *I Learned/I Wonder* Thinksheet is one of the most popular tools we use with primary kids because a question often follows quickly on the heels of new learning. As we review the thinksheets from this lesson, we look for Post-its marked with *L* and any questions that come from that new learning. Sometimes, learners have a question directly related to new information. They may even connect it with an arrow. Other times, learners jot down a question that emerges as they read and explore a topic.

Adapt& Differentiate

This lesson was done with first graders, but here are suggestions for how to adapt and differentiate for the whole range of learners.

First graders place their Post-its on the *I Learned/I Wonder* form. We nudge second graders to write directly on the thinksheet, although if it helps them to organize their thinking to use Post-its when they first try it, they are welcome to do that as well. For kindergarteners, we use a larger 11x17 thinksheet and 3x5 Post-its to give them extra room to draw and write. In this lesson we introduce the notion of wondering. Second graders and many first graders are generally familiar with the term *wonder* and understand that it is related to asking questions. With younger learners and English Language Learners, we often need to spend time modeling what it is to wonder and we teach the language explicitly.

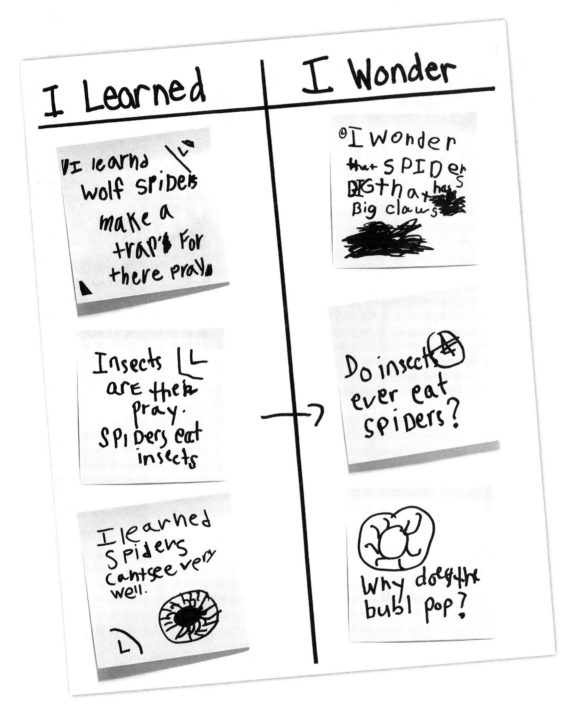

1 This student thought about her new learning and questions as she read. She understood quite well the task at hand. She learned quite a few things, including "Wolf spiders make traps for prey," "Spiders eat insects," and "Spiders can't see very well." She wondered, "Do insects ever eat spiders?" and linked the question with an arrow to new learning: "Spiders eat insects." Linking new learning to a question is a great sign of the evolving thinking that is at the heart of reading comprehension. We might invite her to teach other kids how to use arrows to link thoughts.

Thinksheets

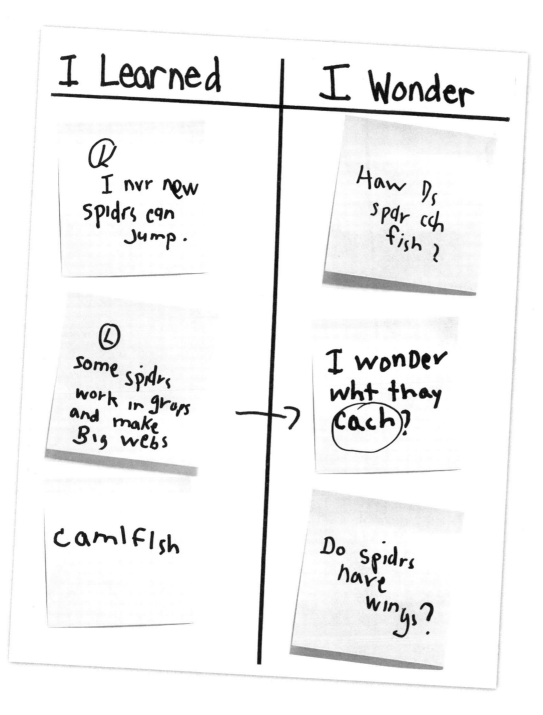

2 This thinksheet shows active reading and learning. The student also connected his question to new learning with an arrow. I was confused by the Post-it in the bottom left-hand corner, so I conferred with the student. He showed me on the *TIME For Kids* "Spiders!" poster where a spider uses camouflage, a concept he already understood, and explained that many animals use camouflage as protection against enemies, not just spiders.

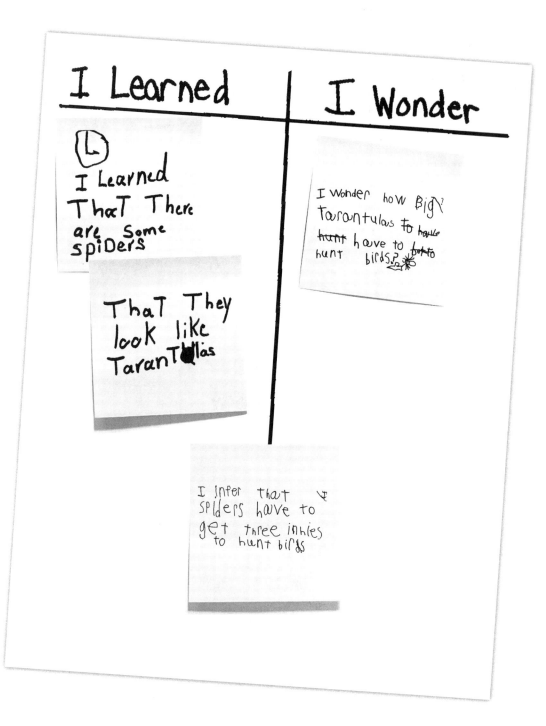

3 Here we see an authentic question: "I wonder how big tarantulas need to be to hunt birds?" Ezekiel attempted to answer his question with an inference: "I infer that spiders have to get to be three inches to hunt birds." I confess that I didn't know that tarantulas could eat birds, so when I read this I thought Ezekiel might have a misconception. I asked Ezekiel to show me where he got that information and, sure enough, he found the information in a book he read. It had a picture of a spider catching a small bird and estimated that the spider was about three inches across. Ezekiel had already learned what it is to infer at an earlier time.

Thinksheets

I Learned	I Wonder
I learned spiders have hooked claws ! that way they don't get stuck in their own webs	

4 This student wrote, "I learned that spiders have hooked claws. That way, they don't get stuck in their own webs." Great learning here! I conferred with the student to see if she wondered anything about it. She wondered if all spiders have these hooked claws. Since I was unsure, I suggested this would be a great time to do a little research. We found another spider book, and I left her poring over the images, looking at spider legs.

I Learned	I Wonder
	Do the claws scratch? Can they hurt you?

5 On this Post-it, the child explained that he learned that spiders can have a claw and he wondered if the claws scratch. I scripted the student's question and together we searched for information. We learned that the claw is too small to harm people, but big enough to help the spider as it climbs around the web.

View and Read to Learn and Wonder
Use images and words to gain understanding

TEACHING MOVES	TEACHING LANGUAGE

Connect and Engage

Engage kids by holding up the book or magazine cover and enthusiastically reading the title aloud.

- Wow! Take a look at this picture! What do you know about...? A lot of you already have some background knowledge (BK) about.... Turn to each other and talk about that.

Record what kids think they know about the topic on the *What We Think We Know/What We Learned* Anchor Chart.

- I want to record some things we think we know about...on this chart. Who wants to share your BK about...? I'll write your ideas on the chart.

Model

Share the two-column *I Learned/ I Wonder* Thinksheet. Explain that sometimes when we learn new information, we wonder about it. Invite kids to respond.

- Today, as I read about...I am going to jot down my new learning on a Post-it. Then I'll put the Post-it on this thinksheet in the *I Learned* column.

- If I wonder something as I read about...I will write what I wonder on a Post-it and put it in the *I Wonder* column.

Respond to a photograph. Show how you think and wonder about images to gain understanding.

- I'm going to look at this photograph. We can get a lot of information from photographs.

- I'm going to show you how I learn and wonder about information as I look at this page. I am really interested in the...and it makes me really wonder what...so I am going to write my question on a Post-it and put it in the *I Wonder* column.

Model for kids how to record learning and wondering on Post-its and place them in the appropriate column of the thinksheet.

- As I read on, I discover...Wow! I never knew that! I'm going to mark my Post-it with an *L* and write down what I learned and put it in the *I Learned* column.

Guide

Engage kids in the process by reading aloud and guiding the discussion.

- Let's try this together. Here is a clipboard and thinksheet with Post-its for each of you. Let's look at the picture of...I'll read what the words say....

Have them record what they learn and wonder on Post-its and then put the Post-its in the appropriate column of the thinksheet.

- If you learned something new in the part I just read, jot it down and draw your new learning. Remember to mark your Post-it with an *L* and put it in the *I Learned* column of the thinksheet.

- If you have anything you wonder, jot it down on a Post-it and put it in the *I Wonder* column of the thinksheet.

The Teaching Moves outline your instructional sequence and the Teaching Language gives you an idea about what to say to your students.

LESSON GUIDE

TEACHING LANGUAGE	TEACHING MOVES

Collaborate

- Read through your copy of the book or article and look carefully at the pictures, noticing and thinking about any new learning you have as well as anything you wonder. Then jot down or draw that information on a Post-it and put it in the matching column on the thinksheet.

Invite kids to join with a partner and continue reading the text and looking at the pictures, jotting their new learning and wondering on their thinksheets.

- I'll be walking around the room, checking in with your groups as you work. Let me know if you need any help!

Move around the room and confer with partners.

Share the Learning

- As you share today, I want you to hold up your thinksheet and read or talk about the drawings on your Post-its that show your new learning and your wondering.

Invite kids to share their new learning as well as anything they wonder.

- After you share, be sure to ask if there are any questions or comments from the rest of the class. Who wants to go first?

- Let's take a look at the Anchor Chart we created before we started the lesson.

Review the *What We Think We Know/What We Learned* Anchor Chart to discover any new thinking and learning.

- What did we discover by reading about…? I think we can change our thinking and write…in the *I Learned* column. Turn and talk. What do you think about that, now that you have read the article? Before we read the article, we thought…and now we have learned that…. Reading can change thinking. So great.

Reflect & Assess

Did your students:

- use text and images to understand?
- think and wonder about new learning?
- jot down new learning and questions on Post-its and then sort them in two columns: *I Learned* and *I Wonder*?
- understand that misconceptions are normal and that learners revise their thinking after reading and listening to additional information?

Wonder about New Information

Text Matters

When teaching kids to question, we choose text that is engaging and spurs wonder. We look for great visual features as well as quality writing because primary kids often have more questions about photographs than they do about the text. In addition, we take care to select text on a topic that is likely to be somewhat unfamiliar to kids. In that way, their questions bubble up to the surface naturally and we can readily capture their wonder.

Resources&Materials

Lesson Text

Recess at 20 Below by Cindy Lou Aillaud (Alaska Northwest Books, 2005) [Available in the Trade Book Pack.]

Classroom Supplies

- Globe
- *Lingering Questions* Anchor Chart
- 3x3 Post-its for students who are more interested in writing
- 3x5 Post-its for students who are more interested in drawing and for marking new learning at the end of the lesson
- Post-its or Post-its Thinksheets [See *Strategy Book 3*, pages 67–68, or the DVD-ROM.]

Student Supplies

- Clipboard with paper and Post-its
- Pencil

Ask questions when you read, listen, and view

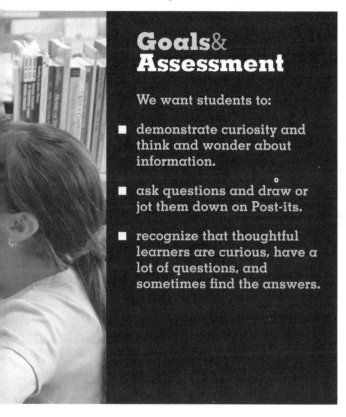

Goals & Assessment

We want students to:

- demonstrate curiosity and think and wonder about information.

- ask questions and draw or jot them down on Post-its.

- recognize that thoughtful learners are curious, have a lot of questions, and sometimes find the answers.

Why & What

Wondering comes naturally to children. Primary kids enter our rooms bursting with questions—*Why is the moon out in daytime? Why do dogs bark?* Questioning is the strategy that propels learners ahead and keeps them coming back for more. Active learners wonder about all sorts of things as they learn. They ask questions to learn new information, to clarify confusion, and to better understand what they view, hear, and read. From the day kids set foot in our classrooms, we nurture their wonder by sharing our own questions as we go. We celebrate kids' curiosity, so they understand right from the get-go that nothing is more important than their questions. We teach them that wondering is at the heart of learning and that all of their questions have value. Learning flourishes when kids believe their questions matter.

How

Connect and Engage

- Share the cover of the book and read the title. Have kids turn and talk about what the book might be about and then share their thoughts.

Model

- Explain that good readers wonder about information and ask questions to understand.

- Explain what it is to be *curious*.

- Jot down or draw questions while reading.

Guide

- Engage kids in the process of writing down their questions.

- Continue reading and sharing questions as kids jot down and draw theirs.

- Stop to share information and answer earlier questions.

- Read the book to the end as kids listen, write, or draw. Stop occasionally to let kids turn and talk about what they wonder.

- Share how we ask questions, read on, and talk to someone to clarify confusion and make sense of text.

Practice Independently

- Review the lesson so kids understand and remember what to do on their own.

- Explain what a *lingering question* is.

- Invite kids to spread out around the room and write or draw lingering questions, new learning, or big ideas.

- Move around the room and confer with kids as they work.

Share the Learning

- Ask kids to share their Post-its and place them on the *Lingering Questions* Anchor Chart.

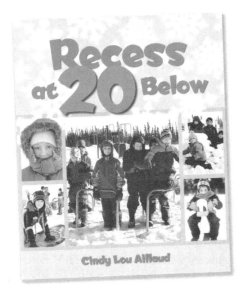

Lesson Text

Recess at 20 Below is a truly captivating narrative written by Cindy Lou Aillaud, an elementary physical-education teacher in Delta Junction, Alaska, a far northern town at the end of the Alaska Highway. The cut-off point for the school's outdoor recess is twenty below zero. Whoa! The story focuses on how cold it can get, how kids cope, and how much fun they have—regardless of the frigid temperature. For most of our kids, this is a fascinating, yet unfamiliar, topic. Unless you happen to live above the Arctic Circle, it is unlikely you would ever have recess at zero, let alone twenty below! The book is chock-full of vivid photographs and interesting, yet unfamiliar, content that spawns curiosity and questions.

From *Recess at 20 Below* by Cindy Lou Aillaud, © 2005, used with permission from Alaska Northwest Books ®, an imprint of Graphic Arts Center Publishing Company.

TEACHING MOVES	TEACHING LANGUAGE

Connect and Engage

Share the cover of the book and read the title. Have kids turn and talk about what the book might be about and then share their thoughts.

Recess at 20 Below. Hmmm, what an interesting title. Take a look at the pictures on the cover. What do you suppose this book is about? Why is it called *Recess at 20 Below?* Turn to each other and talk. *[Kids turn and talk.]*

Devon: I don't know, but twenty below is really cold.

Say more about that, Devon.

Devon: My grandparents live in Wisconsin and we visit them and it gets really cold there.

Do you play outside when it's really cold?

Devon: Not so much. We mostly stay in.

Ginny: Twenty below is way too cold for recess, but it looks like they go out anyway.

I agree. I grew up in a place where once in a while the temperature would drop to twenty degrees below zero and we soooo couldn't go out for recess. Just plain zero is really cold. Twenty below is extremely cold. Most places never even get that cold. But from the title, it sounds like these kids do go out for recess even at twenty below.

[I open the book to the first page and show the drawing of a map of Alaska.] See this map? This is a map of Alaska, where the story takes place. Let me show you where it is on the globe. *[I point to Alaska on the globe.]* Turn and talk: What do you think you already know about Alaska? *[Kids turn and talk.]*

Jason: It's really cold there.

You are right about that, Jason. It's really cold in the winter. As a matter of fact, it gets to twenty below zero or even colder.

Shannon: It's up near the North Pole.

Such good noticing, Shannon. Look on this map. This line is called the Arctic Circle. The town where this story takes place is above the Arctic Circle, where the North Pole is. It gets very cold there.

> Sophie: How do they go to recess if it is so cold?

> Jake: Do they ever have an inside day?

Good questions, you two. I am really curious to find out more about life in such a cold place. Let's see what we discover.

Model

Notice how Sophie was asking a question, "How do they go to recess if it is so cold?" And Jake was wondering: "Do they ever have an inside day?" In the last few lessons we have been noticing and thinking about new information as we read. One thing we have noticed is that when we read new information or see a new photograph, we might wonder something about it.

Explain that good readers wonder about information and ask questions to understand.

Human beings are *curious*. We ask questions about all sorts of things because we want to know more. Curiosity is what leads us to ask questions and learn. I don't know much about places that are so cold, so I am curious to find out more. I will probably have a lot of questions about this story because so much of the information is new to me. Turn to each other and talk: How many of you have questions sometimes when you read a book or listen to a story? How many of you are curious learners? *[Kids turn and talk.]*

Explain what it is to be curious.

I see that many of you have noticed that you have questions when you read or listen. I'm going to show you how it works for me. I am going to jot down my questions on Post-its as I read this story. I might write the words. I might draw what I am wondering and put a question mark next to it. Right here on the cover, I am going to put a question kind of like Sophie's and Jake's: "Why have recess at twenty below zero?" I am also curious: "What would life be like in such a cold place?" So I will write that question down on another Post-it and stick both Post-its right on the cover. Let's keep reading and see what we find out. *[I turn to the first page, with the photo of kids walking to school in darkness, and read.]*

Jot down or draw questions while reading.

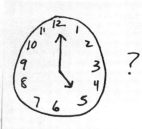

Why have recess at 20° below 0?

What would life be like in such a cold place?

Why are they walking in the night time?

> *The snow on the ground sparkles like diamonds and the air is filled with tiny ice crystals twinkling out of the sky.*

Wow, I love the writing, don't you? I am curious about this photograph. The kids are all dressed, walking somewhere, but it is pitch dark. Why are they walking in the nighttime? What time is it? I am going to draw a clock on this Post-it and then put a question mark next to it. The question mark will remind me that I had a question and the clock will remind me that I was wondering what time it is and why they are walking in the dark. Maybe I will find out as I read on.

[I read the next three pages.]

I didn't get my questions about walking in the dark answered, but I am beginning to get an idea of what life would be like in such a cold place. I am thinking it would be a real pain to have to bundle up like this every day. How long would it take to get all bundled up like this, I wonder? Turn to each other and talk: What do you think? *[Kids turn and talk.]*

Jared: When I go sledding, it takes forever to get dressed.

Alexis: And you can hardly move because of all those clothes.

Interesting, you two. I think it would be really hard to spend all of that time dressing for recess every day. I think a lot of things would be really hard to do if you lived in such a cold place. Daily life would be difficult, getting dressed, getting around, and things like that.

Engage kids in the process of writing down their questions.

Guide

OK, before I start reading again, turn to each other and talk about anything you wonder about this story so far—anything you are curious about. *[Kids turn and talk.]* I am going to give each of you a clipboard, with three large Post-its or six small ones, whichever you choose. If you mostly want to draw what you wonder, choose the bigger Post-its. If you want to write what you wonder, the smaller Post-its might work better. It's up to you. If there is something you are curious about, if you have a question, draw it or write it down on a Post-it. *[Kids write or draw questions on their clipboards.]* Who wants to share something they wonder about? *[Kids either read their writing or use their drawing to express their questions.]*

How do birds keep warm?

How do they drink?

How do people drive?

How do they play sports?

Such interesting questions. I can tell how curious you are. Let's read on and see what else we learn and wonder. *[I continue to read. Kids jot down and draw their questions or just listen as I read. I stop when we get to the picture of the little girl, her tongue, and the swing chain.]* Yikes, this is a scary picture. What is happening? Turn and talk about it. *[Kids turn and talk.]* Any thoughts or questions?

Jeremy: What will happen to her tongue if it touches that chain?

Katie: I know—it will get stuck.

Andrew: And get all bloody.

Interesting thinking. I'm curious about something. I'm wondering how to fix this problem. I'll write that question on a Post-it and then read on to see if I find out. Sometimes when we keep reading, we get our questions answered.

When it's this cold, we have to be careful never to touch our tongue on something metal. It will stick!

Ah, just like Katie said!

Then a teacher will have to use a hair dryer or pour a glass of warm water over it to get your tongue free.

Ricardo: Why would she use a hair dryer?

Good question, Ricardo. What do the rest of you think?

Solange: It is warm.

Say more about that, Solange.

Solange: The tongue gets frozen, and the hair dryer melts it.

Such good thinking. The same goes for the warm water, doesn't it? Pouring warm water where the tongue touches the metal melts the ice and releases the tongue. That's how thinking about questions and reading on give us information. And look at this. I got my question answered. The teacher would have to warm the chain to solve the problem.

[Because this book is long and the kids are generally interested but I sense they could use a break, I stop and the following day pick up the story where we left off.] Let's stop for now and read some more of this book tomorrow. But first, jot down or draw anything else you are curious about. *[I give them time to jot down thoughts on a final Post-it.]* Now turn and talk about the question you just wrote or drew. *[Kids turn and talk.]*

Such great questions today.

[The next day, I begin reading Recess at 20 Below *again. I hand out the clipboards, Post-its, and pencils.]* I am going to start reading *Recess at 20 Below* again. As I read, you can listen, draw, or jot down any questions on Post-its, and I'll share my questions as well. *[I read the page where kids peer out the window.]*

If it's colder than 20 below, we have to stay in for recess.

Listen to that. Jake asked if they ever have an inside day. What did you just hear? When would they have an inside day? Turn and talk about that.

Jake: When it's colder than twenty below.

So when it is twenty-one below, what happens?

Suzi: They have to stay inside, because it is dangerous.

So interesting. There is a temperature that is too cold for kids to be outside in northern Alaska.

[I stop at the page of photos of the setting sun and read.]

Our recess is always at noon because it is the sunniest time of the day in my part of Alaska. It isn't very bright though...more like

How can this problem be fixed?

TIP: Sometimes when we are reading aloud for the purpose of instruction, we do not need to read the whole book. Other times, when kids are really engaged, they may want us to read all of the text. When teaching questioning, many of the questions get answered as we read on, so it is useful to read the entire book. If the text is quite long, we often stop reading halfway through and pick up where we left off on the following day.

Continue reading and sharing questions as kids jot down and draw theirs.

Stop to share information and answer earlier questions.

Read the book to the end as kids listen, write, or draw. Stop occasionally to let kids turn and talk about what they wonder.

Share how we ask questions, read on, and talk to someone to clarify confusion and make sense of text.

TIP: When teaching questioning, kids will begin to notice that sometimes their questions get answered as they read on. We show them how we can mark our Post-its with an *A* for *answer* when we notice that our questions have been answered and how we move the Post-it to the place in the text where our question was answered. See Lesson 10 for more explicit instruction in answering questions.

early evening. The sun rises and sets in just three hours—it barely peeks above our mountains. We come to school and go home in pitch-black dark.

Wow! Look how dark it is. *[I turn back to the first page of the book, point to the photograph, and share the Post-it with the clock and the question mark.]* Remember on the very first page, I drew this clock and asked these questions because I was curious? *Why are they walking at nighttime? What time is it?* Well now I know, in Alaska in winter, it is dark for much of the day. It is only light for three hours around noontime. Seems weird, but that is the way it is in northern Alaska. If you live above the Arctic Circle, it is dark for most of the day during the winter. *[I pick up the globe and point out northern Alaska and the Arctic Circle.]* I'm going to move the Post-it with that question to this page because my question was answered here. I'll even mark it with *A* for *answer* and write down my answer. *[I write* Only light for three hours in winter *on the Post-it and mark A.]*

Let's read the very last page.

It won't be long until the sun will feel a tiny bit warm during recess. Then we'll see our sledding mountain shrink and we'll hear the drip, drip, drip of melting icicles. We'll stow our sleds until next winter and get ready for the Midnight Sun to chase away the darkness. One day, not too far from now, we'll be riding our bikes past 10:00 p.m. 'cause the sun will only go down for three hours. But until then, I love recess at 20 below!

Hmm, interesting. Thoughts or questions? Madison?

Madison: I don't get it. What is the Midnight Sun?

Such a great question. One of the most important reasons to ask a question is when we come to a word or an idea that we don't understand. The best way to clear up any confusion is to ask a question. What do you think? Let's read it again. Sometimes the best way to figure something out is to reread. And let's read it with Madison's question in mind. What is the Midnight Sun? *[I reread the last part].* They are going to get ready for the Midnight Sun to chase away the darkness. They'll be riding bikes past 10:00 at night. What is going on here? Turn to each other and talk. Talking with someone is a great way to figure something out and clear up confusion. *[Kids turn and talk].*

Suzanna: It sounds like it isn't dark at night there.

Why do you say that, Suzanna?

Suzanna: Because they can ride bikes at 10:00 at night.

Great thinking, Suzanna. You know how it was dark much of the time in this book so far. That is because it is winter. In the summer, it is light most of the time. You are right about that. So what is the Midnight Sun?

James: When the sun comes out at midnight?

Yes, in the Arctic Circle, it is light most of the time in the summer. In the winter, it is dark most of the time near the Arctic Circle. Questions can really help us when we don't get it. Such great thinking today!

I still keep wondering about a big idea—that question I wrote at first: *What would life be like in such a cold place?* I think it would be hard, going to school in the dark and bundling all up.

Practice Independently

What an amazing book! *Recess at 20 Below*. Now that we have finished the book, let's stop and think about what we did. I showed you how curious I was to find out more information. I modeled the questions I had as I read, and then I wrote or drew them on Post-its. Then you did the same thing with your questions. Sometimes we got our questions answered, like when Jake asked if they ever had an inside day and we found out that they did. So we learned that good readers are curious and ask questions, and sometimes they find answers. How many of you found some answers to some of your questions? *[Some kids nod.]*

Review the lesson so kids understand and remember what to do on their own.

Often we can read a whole book and still have lots of questions. We call those questions *lingering questions*. Lingering questions are questions we still have even after we have read about something. They are questions that didn't get answered in the book. I have a lingering question. I wondered what life would be like in such a cold place. I have a better idea now. I think life would be hard in such a cold place—hard to do stuff we take for granted, like getting dressed and getting around. Even though I know more, I am still curious about life in such a cold place. Anybody else have a lingering question that they didn't find an answer to? Turn and talk about any lingering questions you have. *[Kids turn and talk.]* OK, let's try something.

Explain what a *lingering question* is.

TIP: You can also write down a big idea that you have after listening to this whole book. A big idea for me in this book is how hard life might be in such a cold place. You can use the big Post-it for a big idea if you like.

Take a minute now, spread out, and think about anything you still wonder about this very cold place where they have recess at twenty degrees below zero. Draw or write your lingering question, what you still wonder, on a Post-it. Or write down something you learned or an idea that answers a question. Then we will share what you learned and wonder.

Invite kids to spread out around the room and write or draw any lingering questions, new learning, or big ideas.

[Kids spread out and write and draw what they wonder on Post-its.] I'll walk around and confer with you if you need help or want to talk.

Move around the room and confer with kids as they work.

Share the Learning

OK, who would like to share something they are still curious about—even after reading the entire book *Recess at 20 Below*? As you share your question, you can come up and put it on the *Lingering Questions* Anchor Chart. *[Kids share a range of questions and place their Post-its on the Anchor Chart.]*

Ask kids to share their Post-its and place them on the *Lingering Questions* Anchor Chart.

Sarah: How do they get around, I wonder?

Alexis: Why do they live there when it is so cold?

Ricardo: Why can't they have snowball fights?

Jake: How do animals stay warm and survive?

Such interesting questions. Take a look at these questions on the Anchor Chart; then turn to each other, and talk about what you learned and what you still wonder. If you have some ideas that might answer some of these lingering questions, talk about them. Or you can talk about any new learning you have from reading this book. *[Kids turn and talk about their questions and ideas.]*

When we are curious and think about the questions we have, we learn more when we listen, look at the pictures, and read. If anyone wants to investigate more about life in such a cold place, let me know. We can form a small inquiry group of kids who are interested in learning more about the ideas in *Recess at 20 Below*. Great wondering today, all of you!

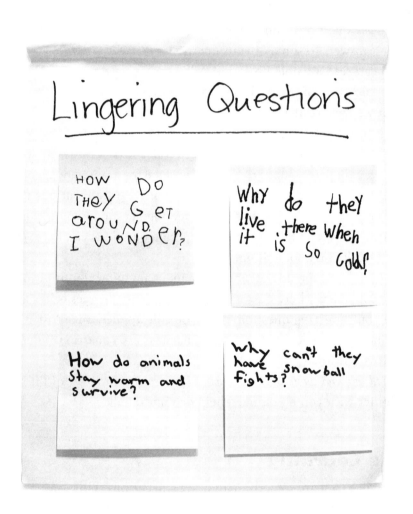

Did your students:

- demonstrate curiosity, think and wonder about information?

- ask questions and draw or jot them down on Post-its?

- recognize that thoughtful learners are curious, have a lot of questions, and sometimes find the answers?

Reflect& Assess

As I review the Post-its, I am looking to see if the kids are writing down or drawing questions they wonder about. I am also looking to see if they answered some of their questions and jotted an *A* for *answer*. When kids read with a question in mind, they are far more likely to notice when that question gets answered. Some questions lead to others, and I notice that as well. Emergent readers often draw their thinking. I check whether they have marked their drawings with a question mark. If they have, it can be an indication that they are thinking about their question as they listen or read.

Adapt& Differentiate

This lesson was done with second graders, but here are suggestions for how to adapt and differentiate for the whole range of learners.

Each second grader had a sheet of paper with 3x3 Post-its for their questions and wonderings and one 3x5 Post-it for an overall response to the book, a new learning, an answer to a question, or a big idea about the story. Some of the kids just wrote questions. Most jotted answers when they found them and wrote their new learning. Some even came up with a big idea about a lingering question.

When we do this lesson with kindergarteners or younger kids, we give them a sheet of paper with three 3x5 Post-its, which gives them more room to draw and write. Some may choose to use 3x3 Post-its. Additionally, when doing this lesson with younger kids, we emphasize simply wondering about information and asking questions. If they find an answer, that's a bonus. When doing this lesson with kindergarteners, we are less likely to ask them to come up with a big idea or a lingering question at the end of the reading. We want them to focus on asking questions and getting used to the idea of wondering about information throughout the text. We don't ignore their attempts at answers, however, and we search for answers as they read, because most kids really want to know the answers to their questions. Our follow-up discussions often focus on finding ways to answer their questions, including doing further research.

I would'nt be able to live in Alaska because I don't like the cold.
How do they got around?

When there eylashes freeze they look glittery why?

It is probaly very inconvinet to catch a flight out of Alaska.
Let's write a Houston vershun!

What is the midnight sun?
The midnight sun is when the sun comes up at 11 pmr.
(A)

If you have an expander or braces would'nt it stick?

Life in such a cold place would be very inconvenient for peoples needs and transporlation also for like electricty and water.
(L)

1 Holly had quite a few thoughtful questions. She asked what the Midnight Sun is and then answered her question by listening to the text. She hit the target when she wrote that life would be inconvenient. She supported this idea with questions, such as "How do they get around?" Holly even suggested a Houston, Texas, version of the book: *Recess at 100 Above!*

Responses by Second Graders

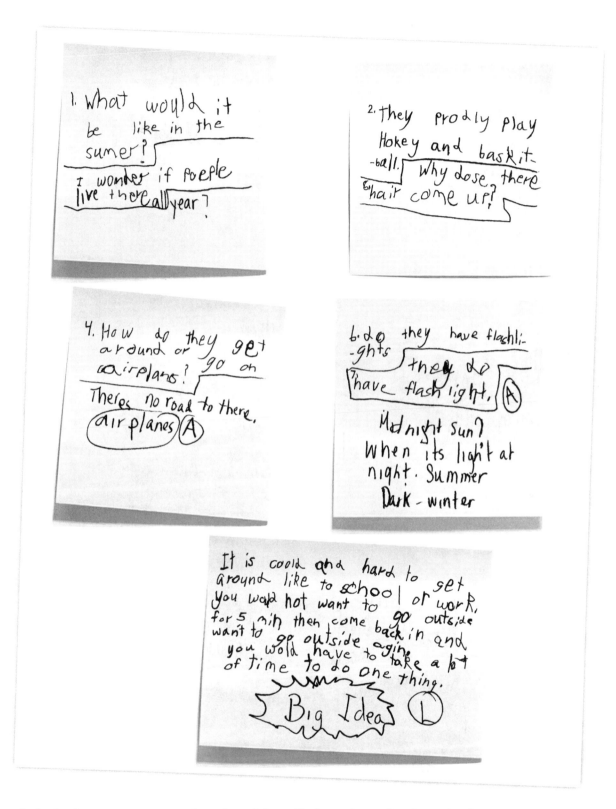

1. What would it be like in the sumer?

I wonder if poeple live there all year?

2. they prodly play Hokey and baskit-ball. Why dose there hair come up?

4. How do they get around or go on airplans?

Theres no road to there.

(airplanes) (A)

6. do they have flashlights they do have flash light. (A)

Midnight Sun? When its light at night. Summer

Dark - winter

It is coold and hard to get around like to school or work. You wold not want to go outside for 5 min then come back in and want to go outside agin you wold have to take a lot of time to do one thing.

Big Idea (I)

2 Andre had many questions and numbered them. He figured out what the midnight sun is: "Light in summer and dark in winter." He marked his large Post-it "Big Idea" and wrote that life would be hard, coming in and going out and back in again! He listened to the story with his questions in mind and marked an *A* when he heard an answer.

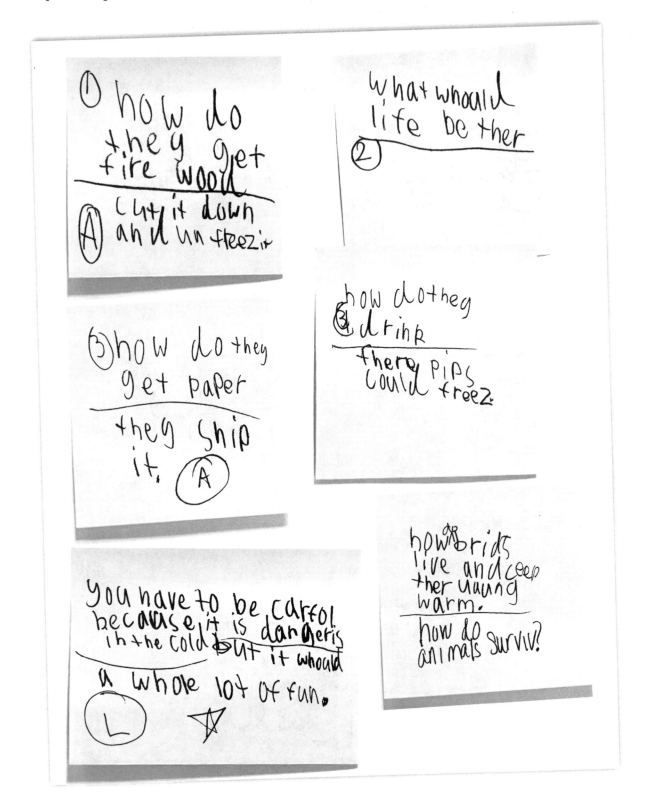

① how do they get fire wood
Ⓐ cut it down and un freezit

what whoald life be ther ②

③ how do they get paper
they ship it, Ⓐ

how do they drihk
there pips could freez.

you have to be carfol because it is dangeris in the cold but it whoald a whole lot of fun.
Ⓛ ☆

how brids live and ceep ther uaung warm.
how do animals surviv?

3 Zeke asked lots of questions and answered several. One particularly interesting question is "How do birds live and keep their young warm?" Zeke followed that line of thinking with an even bigger question: "How do animals survive?" He recognized that people have to be careful living in such a cold place but thought that it would be a whole lot of fun.

Responses by Kindergarteners

4 Gabe drew his questions. I wrote them for him and we discussed them. As he asked questions, we talked about possible answers. We talked about the text where it says that the snow is too dry for snowballs. We also talked about why the sun is out at night and how people shut their curtains to keep the sun out of their eyes when sleeping. Gabe suggested that they must have dark shades to keep all that light out.

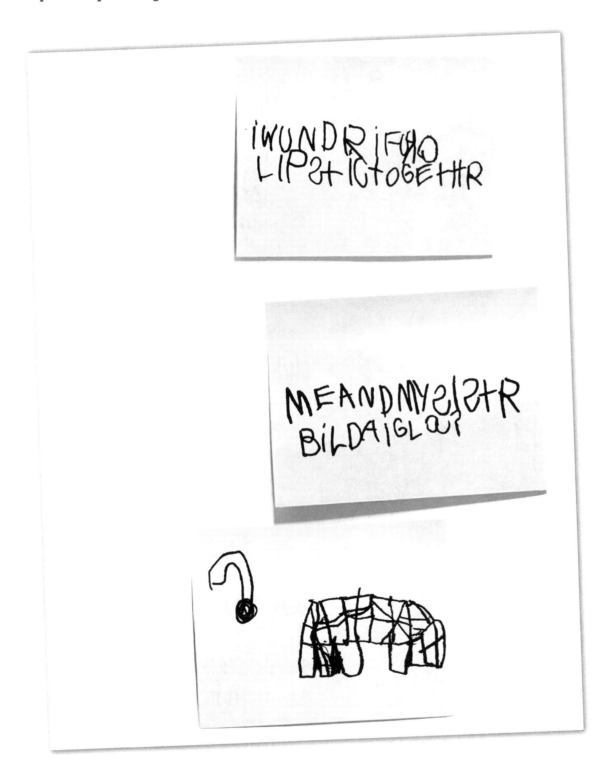

5 Samantha wondered if your lips would stick together in really cold weather. She was fascinated by the picture in the book where the little girl almost puts her tongue on the freezing cold chain. On the second Post-it, Samantha wrote that she and her sister want to build an igloo. When I asked her about her question mark next to the igloo, she explained that she wondered how an igloo could keep you warm. Great question for further research!

Responses by Kindergarteners

6 Hannah drew some questions and wrote others. "Can they snowboard? How do they get rid of the snow? How big is a moose?" She also wrote questions in the right-hand column about the idea of night and day in the Arctic climate. She asked why it is sometimes dark and sometimes light, why the sun is out at night, and whether it is night when they wake up. These questions focus on a great topic for further research. And I would nudge and support her to investigate.

Wonder about New Information

Ask questions when you read, listen, and view

TEACHING MOVES	TEACHING LANGUAGE

Connect and Engage

Share the cover of the book and read the title. Have kids turn and talk about what the book might be about and then share their thoughts.

- Let me read the title to you. Hmmm, that's an interesting one. Take a look at the pictures on the cover. What do you suppose this book is about? Turn and talk about it.

Model

Explain that good readers wonder about information and ask questions to understand.

- In the last few lessons we have noticed that when we read new information or see a new photograph, we might wonder about it.

Explain what it is to be *curious*.

- Humans ask questions about all sorts of things because we want to know more, because we are *curious*. I am curious to find out more about.... Turn to each other and talk about what you are curious about.

Jot down or draw questions while reading.

- As I read this book, I am going to jot down and draw questions when I meet new information.

- Right here, I am curious about.... So I will write that question down on a Post-it and place it right on the book, where my question came up.

Guide

Engage kids in the process of writing down their questions.

- Before I start reading again, turn and talk about anything you wonder about this story.

- On the clipboard and Post-its you have, draw or write what you wonder.

Continue reading and sharing questions as kids jot down and draw theirs.

- As I continue to read, you can listen and draw or jot down any questions on Post-its.

Stop to share information and answer earlier questions.

- What did you just hear me read? What happened? Turn and talk about that.

- Remember on the first page that I wrote a question on a Post-it because I was curious about...? Well, now I know that...I'm going to move the Post-it with that question to this page because my question is answered here. I'll mark it with an *A* for *answer* and write down the answer I found.

The Teaching Moves outline your instructional sequence and the Teaching Language gives you an idea about what to say to your students.

TEACHING LANGUAGE	TEACHING MOVES

Guide

- Let's finish this book now. Keep writing and drawing what you wonder. I'll stop now and then so you can share your thoughts.

Read the book to the end as kids listen, write, or draw. Stop occasionally to let kids turn and talk about what they wonder.

- The best way to clear up confusion is to ask a question. Sometimes the best way to answer your question is to reread. Talking to someone is another great way to figure something out when you are confused.

Share how we ask questions, read on, and talk to someone to clarify confusion and make sense of text.

Practice Independently

- Let's stop and review what we just did. First I showed you how I write down what I'm wondering on Post-its when I read new information. Then you did the same thing with your questions.

Review the lesson so kids understand and remember what to do on their own.

- When we read a whole book and still have questions that didn't get answered, we call them *lingering questions*. I had a question from this book that didn't get answered. How many of you have lingering questions?

Explain what a *lingering question* is.

- OK, now you take a minute and draw or write anything you still wonder about…. Draw or write your lingering questions. Or you can draw or write about any new information or big ideas you got from the book.

Invite kids to spread out around the room and write or draw lingering questions, new learning, or big ideas.

- I'll walk around and confer with you if you need help or want to talk.

Move around the room and confer with kids as they work.

Share the Learning

- Who would like to share something they are still curious about, even after reading all of…? As you share, come up and put your Post-it on the Anchor Chart.

Ask kids to share their Post-its and place them on the *Lingering Questions* Anchor Chart.

Reflect & Assess

Did your students:

- demonstrate curiosity, think and wonder about information?
- ask questions and draw or jot them down on Post-its?
- recognize that thoughtful learners are curious, have a lot of questions, and sometimes find the answers?

Use Questions as Tools for Learning

Text Matters

Many topics can spark kids' questions. Information can be straightforward or a bit puzzling. In either case, the more we learn, the more we wonder. Nonfiction books that have photos or pictures with short captions are particularly good for this lesson. Headings on each page or across a page spread help kids to navigate nonfiction. A few sentences on a page rather than long paragraphs of text are more accessible for kids who are just beginning to learn to find answers to their questions. With just right, accessible text, kids are less likely to get lost in a sea of information.

Resources & Materials

Lesson Text

Biggest, Strongest, Fastest by Steve Jenkins (Houghton Mifflin Company, 1995) [Available in the Trade Book Pack.]

Additional Text

A selection of magazines and a wide variety of nonfiction books on many topics

Classroom Supplies

- *Questions/Answers* Anchor Chart
- Post-its or Post-it Thinksheets [See *Strategy Book 3*, pages 67-68, or the DVD-ROM.]

Student Supplies

- *Questions/Answers* Thinksheet [See *Strategy Book 3*, page 70, or the DVD-ROM.]
- Post-its
- Clipboard
- Pencil

Understand why some questions are answered and some are not

Goals & Assessment

We want students to:

- stop, wonder, and keep a question in mind to try to answer.

- learn strategies for answering questions, including gaining information from pictures as well as text and talking with peers.

- keep track of questions to be investigated but realize that not all questions are answered.

Why & What

Once kids learn that asking questions is what good readers do, there's no stopping them! When we are reading to learn, sometimes our questions are answered and sometimes they are not. When readers stop for a moment to ask a question, we teach them to keep their question in mind and continue reading. As they read on, they often encounter additional information that answers their question. Reading and viewing the pictures and words in the text often provide the information kids are looking for. But when questions are not answered, kids need strategies for going beyond the text to find answers. We teach kids that talking with someone and sharing information is another way to find answers to questions. But most importantly, kids learn that it's a fact of life that not all questions are easily answered or fully resolved.

How

Connect and Engage

- Connect to Lesson 9 on stopping to wonder and asking a question.

- Engage kids with the text by looking at the cover picture.

Model

- Show how to stop to ask a question and pay attention to your inner voice as you read and view the pictures.

- Write a question on a large Post-it. Read on and stop at the information that answers the question.

- Ask kids to share what they noticed you doing as you modeled.

Guide

- Write questions and answers on Post-its and place them on the *Questions/Answers* Anchor Chart.

- Remind kids to ask questions when they don't understand something or are confused.

- Explain that a reader can discuss the information with someone else to answer a question.

Collaborate or Practice Independently

- Invite kids to choose books and use Post-its or the thinksheet to jot down questions and search for answers as they read.

- Move around the room, conferring with kids.

- Discuss how pictures as well as words can provide information that answers a question.

- Confer with individual students to correct misconceptions.

Share the Learning

- Invite kids to share their questions and answers.

- Share the fact that readers do not always find an answer to their question.

- Wrap up by suggesting that kids keep questions in mind—and continue to investigate them.

- Create an Anchor Chart of ways to answer questions.

Lesson Text

Steve Jenkins's picture book *Biggest, Strongest, Fastest* is accessible and interesting to kids because of its compelling illustrations and simple text. Information such as *A blue whale is the largest animal that ever lived* invites questions and whets kids' curiosity. An additional paragraph of information about the animal in a smaller font accompanies the "big fact" and illustration. Sometimes these paragraphs answer the readers' questions; sometimes they don't. The striking collage illustrations and straightforward facts engage the youngest readers. The additional paragraph of information surprises and piques the interest of more developed readers.

Excerpt from *Biggest, Strongest, Fastest* by Steve Jenkins. Copyright © 1995 by Steve Jenkins. Reprinted by permission of Houghton Mifflin Company. All rights reserved.

TEACHING MOVES	TEACHING LANGUAGE

Connect and Engage

Connect to Lesson 9 on stopping to wonder and asking a question.

Today we are going to do something that I know you all love to do; we're going to continue to ask questions as we read. I noticed that you are such curious learners—you want to find out about all kinds of things. Often the more we learn, the more we wonder. I've heard you ask some really interesting questions as you stopped to wonder about the information you read. Sometimes information is brand-new so you want to know more. Today we'll mark the text with a Post-it and draw and write a question when one pops into our minds as we read.

Engage kids with the text by looking at the cover picture.

Thoughtful readers always ask questions when they read. We'll learn how to answer the questions we ask. Let's take a look at this book called *Biggest, Strongest, Fastest.* Look at the cover picture of the cheetah for a moment. I can see that some of you are so curious about this cheetah! Turn and talk about what you are thinking and any questions you have about this cheetah. *[I call on kids to share.]*

> Katie: How fast can he run?
>
> Owen: What is he chasing?

These are great questions! This cheetah sure looks like it's moving, even in the picture. And Owen, tell us more about your question.

> Owen: I think he's chasing something. Maybe he's hunting and he wants to eat. I wonder what animal he is trying to catch.

So thoughtful. This is exactly what we'll be doing today. We'll be learning information from both the pictures and the words, and then we'll stop and wonder about it. We'll see if we can find answers to our questions. Keep your questions in mind, and we'll see if we can answer them after we do some reading.

Model

Now I want you to watch me as I read the words and view the pictures. I'm going to pay attention to my inner voice. Please listen to what I say and watch what I do. I'll ask you to tell me what you noticed in a few minutes. Here we go. *[I open to page 1.]* I'm going to look at this picture before I read the page. Wow—look at this giraffe! *[I read.]*

> *The tallest animal is the giraffe.*

Gosh, right now I hear my inner voice asking a question. I'm wondering "How tall are giraffes?" I'm sharing my question out loud with you all, but when I'm reading on my own, it's my inner voice that is asking the question.

Now I'm going to write my question on a Post-it: *How tall are giraffes?* I will hold on to my Post-it and see if I come to information that answers my question.

I'm going to read this bit of text over here, next to the giraffe:

> *Male giraffes grow as tall as 19 feet.*

That's incredible! Nineteen feet is much, much taller than this ceiling! I found an answer to my question, so I put my Post-it right next to the information I found. Then I'll draw a line under my question on the Post-it and write *19 feet tall.*

Now, turn and talk about what you just saw me do. *[Kids turn and talk, then share as a whole group.]*

> Jonathan: You stopped and wrote down your question about the giraffe.
>
> Jeannie: You noticed how tall it is, then you wrote the answer.
>
> Marissa: You put your question right by the answer.
>
> Valerie: It didn't take long to answer that question!

And Valerie, you are so right; it didn't take long to answer that question. But it's not always so quick or so easy. Good observing! I did stop to write down my question, I put my Post-it in the book next to the information that answered my question, and I wrote down the information that answered my question. *[I write what the kids noticed me doing in a notebook to use for an Anchor Chart later on.]*

Show how to stop to ask a question and pay attention to your inner voice as you read and view the pictures.

Write a question on a large Post-it. Read on and stop at the information that answers the question.

Ask kids to share what they noticed you doing as you modeled.

TIP: We jot kids' thinking in a notebook to later create an Anchor Chart of their thinking.

Guide

Let's do the next one together. Wow! Look at the picture of the huge snake. Let's read about it:

> *There are many kinds of large snakes, but the anaconda is the biggest.*

I'm wondering: How big is that anaconda? Let's see if you have any other questions. Turn and talk about any questions you have. Then we'll share some of them.

Write questions and answers on Post-its and place them on the Questions/Answers Anchor Chart.

Questions	Answers
How big is it (the anaconda)?	Anaconda – 25 feet long! Weighs 400 pounds!
Does it squeeze its prey to kill it?	
What does it eat?	

Josh: How big is it?

Karey: Does it squeeze its prey to kill it?

Amy: What does it eat?

I'm going to write these questions on Post-its. Then I'll put them up here on our Anchor Chart that has a column for Questions and one for Answers. Let's keep reading to see if we find an answer to any of these questions:

Anacondas can grow to be over 25 feet long and weigh 400 pounds.

Josh: Whoa! 25 feet—I never knew they were that big!

Good for you, Josh. You used the words "I never knew" to show that it is new information for you. This information answers our question. I'll write that information on another Post-it and put it in the Answer column. *[I write* 25 feet long, weighs 400 pounds *on a Post-it and put it on the Anchor Chart.]*

Marissa: That's one big snake!

Great response. You are reacting to this amazing information, Marissa. But let's go back to Karey's and Amy's questions, which I wrote on these Post-its: *Does it squeeze its prey to kill it?* and *What does it eat?* These are interesting questions. I'm going to keep reading, and I want you to listen carefully to see if we find information that answers these questions. Let me know if you hear information that answers either of these two questions. *[I read.]*

They wait in trees and drop onto their prey. A hungry anaconda can swallow a whole deer or goat.

Amy: That's it! They eat deer and even goats!

OK, Amy. Good listening! You heard me read information that answered your question about what the anaconda eats. I'm going to stick a Post-it here to mark the place where we found the answer. But instead of me writing, would you write the answer—that it eats deer and goats—on a Post-it for us? And then we'll put your answer next to your question on the Anchor Chart.

How about your question, Karey? Let's reread a bit.

They wait in trees and drop onto their prey.

Turn and talk: Do we have information that answers Karey's question: Does the anaconda squeeze its prey?

Jonathan: I don't understand. It didn't say anything about squeezing. Does it really kill an animal by squeezing it?

Good question. It's a good idea to ask a question when we are confused or don't understand something.

Remind kids to ask questions when they don't understand something or are confused.

Jonathan: It just said that the anaconda drops down onto its prey from the trees. It's confusing. It didn't say if it bites the prey, squeezes it, or kills it in some other way.

Mariana: I think anacondas bite their prey to kill it.

I'm going to ask everyone: What should we do if we don't understand something?

[Kids shout out.] Ask a question!

Exactly. So let's keep Jonathan and Karey's question in mind and keep reading to see if we learn more about this and clear up our confusion.

José: I saw a picture of an anaconda wrapped around a caiman, like an alligator. So I think it does squeeze its prey.

Interesting information, José. What do you think, Karey? Jonathan? Does José's information help to answer your question? *[They nod.]*

We would want to check out this information.

José: I'll go get the book.

[José returns with the book and shows the photo of the anaconda wrapped around a caiman.] Look at this picture, everyone. This confirms what José told us about the anaconda squeezing its prey. This is so important. By talking to José and viewing this photograph, we have more information—that anacondas squeeze their prey. Maybe we can check out whether it bites, Mariana. I'll come talk with you about this, and we'll look for more information. Now we have learned that sometimes we can figure out an answer to a question by talking with someone about it. This is pretty exciting. You all can teach each other information.

TIP: We can't stress enough how important it is to encourage kids to ask a question when they are confused or don't understand something. Sometimes a child will say something that may be inaccurate—a misconception. Then we discuss the information or confer with the child individually to address the confusion.

Explain that a reader can discuss the information with someone else to answer a question.

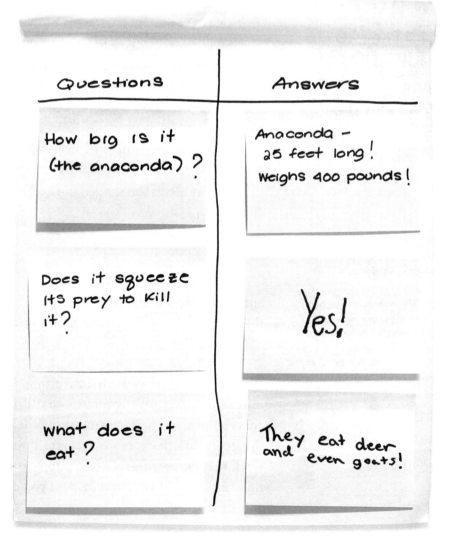

Collaborate or Practice Independently

Invite kids to choose books and use Post-its or the thinksheet to jot down questions and search for answers as they read.

Now it's your turn to go off and try this on your own. You may work by yourself or with a partner. You know that there are bins of books on the tables, and you can choose one of these to read. And there are Post-its and pencils on each table, too. If you decide to work on the floor up here, there are some bins of books here. You'll need to take a clipboard and use Post-its or the *Questions/Answers* Thinksheet to record your thinking. Have fun!

[Kids work independently and with partners as I circulate. I notice Javier and Ernesto using a picture to answer their question about a tortoise. I confer with them about this.]

Move around the room, conferring with kids.

How's it going?

Javier: We are looking at this tortoise that lives in the desert.

Ernesto: We wondered, "Why is the tortoise in the hole?" We didn't know tortoises got into holes.

Discuss how pictures as well as words can provide information that answers a question.

Interesting question, you two. I see you have an answer underneath your question. Will you read your answer?

Javier: We looked at the picture and saw that the tortoise is in the desert. We know the desert is hot. So we thought maybe the tortoise went into the hole to get out of the sun.

So you wrote *Maybe to get out of the sun*. That's really good thinking, and you used the photograph of the desert to help you. You know the desert is a hot place, and you noticed the dark hole, where the tortoise could get out of the sun. So that is a reasonable conclusion. Let's see if the words in the caption help us: "A desert tortoise goes into a hole to keep cool."

So great! The words confirm what you learned from the clues in the photo. Sometimes both the words and the pictures help us answer a question.

Ernesto: So the tortoise gets out of the sun *and* stays cool!

Exactly.

[I next confer with Mariana about the misconception she expressed during the lesson.]

Confer with individual students to correct misconceptions.

Mariana, look here. Maybe this book will give us more information about anacondas and whether they bite. Here's that picture José shared. Let's read the caption. It says, *Anacondas squeeze their prey and then they swallow it whole.*

TIP: Misconceptions happen. And young kids have a lot of them. To avoid embarrassing kids, we often correct misinformation in a conference rather than in front of the whole group.

Mariana: Wow! So it does squeeze it, not bite it. I didn't know that. And it can swallow an animal whole!

Exactly. This is such interesting information. When we have some information that isn't accurate, we call that a *misconception*. You had a misconception about how anacondas kill their food. And now you learned something new and have more accurate information! Would you be willing to teach that big word—misconception—to the whole class? I think it's something kids should know about. And you can teach them the new information you learned, too, OK?

Mariana: Sure!

Share the Learning

[I bring the kids together and ask them to share how they answered their questions (or not).]

Invite kids to share their questions and answers.

Katie and Owen, did you find any answers to your questions?

Katie: I learned that cheetahs can run as fast as a car or bus, but not for very long; they get tired.

Owen: I don't know what animal the cheetah in that picture is chasing. It's just the cheetah.

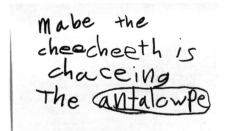

Good for you two for keeping your questions in mind and trying to answer them. Sometimes we can find the answer to a question and sometimes we can't. That's OK. But go ahead and write down your thinking on a Post-it.

Share the fact that readers do not always find an answer to their question.

Marissa: I read that cheetahs like to eat antelope, but there isn't one in the picture.

That's interesting information, Marissa. By talking to Marissa, we found out some information—that cheetahs like to eat antelope.

Owen: So maybe the cheetah is chasing an antelope!

How about if you and Marissa work together to find out more information about this? You can do some research!

Mariana learned something really important. She's going to share it with you now. What was that word, Mariana?

Wrap up by suggesting that kids keep questions in mind—and continue to investigate them.

Mariana: Misconception—I had a misconception. I thought anacondas bit their food, then I learned something different. They don't bite their food; they squeeze it, like José said. And then I learned that they swallow their food whole!

TIP: When kids learn something new, we ask them to share it with the whole group. It's empowering for them to teach their peers.

Great teaching, Mariana! You taught us about a misconception—that's when we don't have accurate information. Now we learned an important word from you, and we also learned some amazing information—that anacondas swallow their food whole! Thanks for teaching us this.

Let's review some of the ways we learned to answer our questions. I'll write down what you say, and then I'll can make an Anchor Chart to guide us as we ask and answer questions.

Create an Anchor Chart of ways to answer questions.

[Kids share out, and I record their thinking on the chart.]

Did your students:

■ stop, wonder, and keep a question in mind to try to answer it?

■ learn strategies for answering questions, including gaining information from pictures as well as text and talking with peers?

■ keep track of questions to be investigated but realize that not all questions are answered?

Reflect& Assess

The most important thing we can do when teaching kids to seek answers to questions is to listen to their questions and let them take the lead in exploring them. We listen closely as we confer with kids and guide them to think through the text information and uncover information that takes their thinking further. It's not about finding the "one and only one" correct answer to a question, but we do want kids to gain accurate information as they read. If kids have confused ideas or misconceptions, we try to catch them and help kids to correct them. We can't always answer every question, but it's the process of wondering and seeking information that is both fun and interesting.

Adapt& Differentiate

This lesson was done with first graders, but here are suggestions for how to adapt and differentiate for the whole range of learners.

Most kids wrote and drew answers to their questions on Post-its. Many elaborated orally on the information they found but did not put all their thinking into writing. As kids become more proficient at writing, they are better able to capture their thinking in written responses. More developed readers and writers can write their questions on the *Questions/Answers* Thinksheet.

For emergent readers, the entire lesson can be done with pictures and photographs. Pictures and photographs are often so loaded with information that they can stand on their own as sources for asking and often answering questions. Wordless picture books, too, can prompt emergent readers to wonder. They can "read" and learn information from the pictures alone. Kids can learn this way of thinking without reading words. Asking a question and finding the answer by viewing information and drawing a response tell kids that they can wonder and think about information even as they learn to read words.

The language on the chart constructed at the end of the lesson (see page 43, top left) works well with first and second graders. With a kindergarten class, we would construct a simpler Anchor Chart (seen here on the right). As we remind kids of ways to find answers to their questions, we sketch a visual reminder for each bullet.

When we Read with a Question in Mind

① We read the text and view the pictures to see if we can answer our question.

② We talk to someone who shares their background knowledge with us.

③ We realize that we can't always answer our questions.

How Do We Find Answers to our Questions?

• Look at pictures

• Talk to someone

• Read and listen

First-Grade Responses

1 Partners Sammy and Leo asked a question about chameleons: "I wonder why chameleons change colors?" Leo couldn't resist sharing his amazement, saying "I never knew chameleons change colors!"

They wrote their first two ideas, and I listened as the discussion continued.

Sammy: I bet they change colors to camouflage—then nothing can see them.

Leo: I get it—then they wouldn't get eaten!

We listen carefully to kids' conversations, noting when they add to their thinking as Leo and Sammy did. They often discuss more sophisticated ideas than they are able to record in writing. We assess young children's oral language as well as their drawing and writing to get a more complete picture of what they understand.

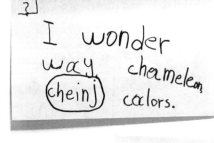

I wonder way chameleon (chein) colors.

I never knew chameleon's chang color's.

I wonder why boa's (sqeeze) there prey.

2 I found out from talking with this child that she was confused about the fact that boas constrict to kill their prey. She assumed boas killed their food by biting it, hence her question. Kids' questions allow us to help them clarify misconceptions, so I would confer with her and reiterate the information we learned in the lesson—that boas squeeze their prey to kill it so they can then eat it.

Second-Grade Responses

1 When this child learned that anacondas can be twenty-five feet long, he made an immediate comparison by asking his teacher how tall she was! He was amazed and sketched his comparison. He thought further and realized that "The anaconda is 20 feet longer than my teacher Lynne because my teacher is five feet tall." Amazing information to be sure, and kudos to kids who reason through information in this way to arrive at a fuller understanding of it.

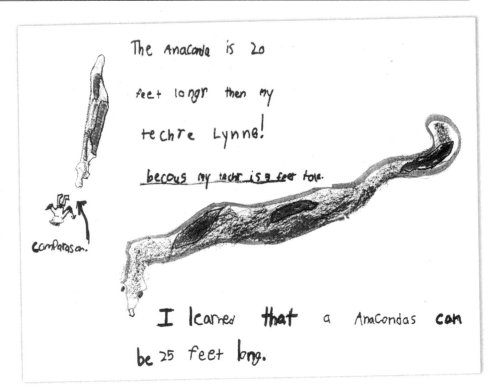

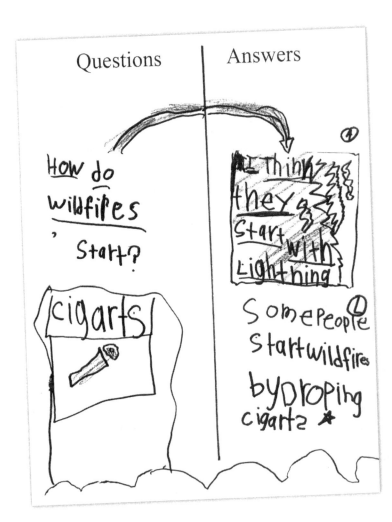

2 Kiki was reading and learning about wildfires. She asked a question, "How do wildfires start?" and then began to read to answer it. Kiki realized that she could draw an arrow connecting her question with her answer, "I think they start with lightning." Then she read some startling information—that people can start wildfires by dropping a cigarette. In a conference, Kiki and I discussed the fact that there can be more than one answer to a question.

3 Kimberly organized her questions about cats all on her own. She encountered information that answered her initial question, wondering if cats always land on their feet. She kept reading and found out more information that not only answered her question but extended her thinking—finding out that cats rotate their bodies to land on their feet. When kids work independently to ask authentic questions such as this one and organize information on their own, they are well on their way to using questions as tools for research and investigation.

Use Questions as Tools for Learning

Understand why some questions are answered and some are not

TEACHING MOVES	TEACHING LANGUAGE
	Connect and Engage
Connect to Lesson 9 on stopping to wonder and asking a question.	■ We're going to continue to ask questions as we read. I think it's true that the more we learn, the more we wonder.
	■ Thoughtful readers are curious, and they often ask questions when they read or view information.
Engage kids with the text by looking at the cover picture.	■ Turn and talk about something that you wonder about this.
	Model
Show how to stop to ask a question and pay attention to your inner voice as you read and view the pictures.	■ Notice what you see me doing as I read the words and view the pictures. I'll ask you to tell me what you noticed in a few minutes.
Write a question on a large Post-it. Read on and stop at the information that answers the question.	■ I'm going to write my question on the Post-it and see if I come to some information that answers my question while I read.
	■ I found an answer to my question, and I'm going to put my Post-it right next to it. And then draw a line under my question and write...
Ask kids to share what they noticed you doing as you modeled.	■ Turn and talk about what you just saw me do.... Yes! Good noticing. I did all those things.
	Guide
Write questions and answers on Post-its and place them on the *Questions/Answers* Anchor Chart.	■ Let's read on, and when we have questions, we'll write them on Post-its and place them on this chart. Here we go...this information answers our question!
Remind kids to ask questions when they don't understand something or are confused.	■ Sometimes we can ask a question when we don't understand or are confused. Let's keep this question in mind as we read.
Explain that a reader can discuss the information with someone else to answer a question.	■ Now we've learned that sometimes we can figure out an answer to our question by talking with someone. We can share information we find out to answer our question. That's exciting! You can all teach each other.

The Teaching Moves outline your instructional sequence and the
Teaching Language gives you an idea about what to say to your students.

TEACHING LANGUAGE	TEACHING MOVES

Collaborate or Practice Independently

- Now it's your turn to go off and try this on your own. You may work by yourself or with a partner.

  Invite kids to choose books and use Post-its or the thinksheet to jot down questions and search for answers as they read.

- How's it going? Do you have some good questions? How are you trying to find answers?

  Move around the room, conferring with kids.

- You did a great job! The words confirm what you noticed in the photo so you were able to answer your question.

  Discuss how pictures as well as words can provide information that answers a question.

- You had a misconception about...and now you have learned something new and have more accurate information.

  Confer with individual students to correct misconceptions.

Share the Learning

- Let's share out some of your questions. You worked hard trying to find some answers.

  Invite kids to share their questions and answers.

- Good for you for keeping your question in mind and trying to find the answer. Sometimes we can find the answers to our questions, and sometimes we can't.

  Share the fact that readers do not always find an answer to their question.

- We can keep our questions in mind. Let's review some of the ways we can discover answers to our questions, and we'll make a chart to guide us as we read with our questions in mind.

  Wrap up by suggesting that kids keep questions in mind—and continue to investigate them.

  Create an Anchor Chart of ways to answer questions.

Reflect & Assess

Did your students:

- stop, wonder, and keep a question in mind to try to answer it?

- learn strategies for answering questions, including gaining information from pictures as well as text and talking with peers?

- keep track of questions to be investigated but realize that not all questions are answered?

Read with a
Question in Mind

Text Matters

As we read to answer a question, we often encounter a wealth of information in relation to it. Using straightforward expository text provides kids with opportunities to find the information they need to answer a question. For this lesson, we choose text that incorporates prominent navigational features, such as clear headings, a table of contents, and an index, as well as solid, factual information. We show kids how to take brief notes on information to answer a question. So as you choose additional texts for this lesson, look for a variety of visual and text features that support kids in their quest for information. And don't forget to check for a table of contents. Not all books have one!

Resources & Materials

Lesson Text

Tornado by Catherine Chambers (Heinemann Library, 2007) [Available in the Trade Book Pack.]

Additional Texts

Books about tornadoes and other weather events, or a variety of nonfiction texts

Classroom Supplies

- *I Wonder/I Learned* Anchor Chart and marker
- Post-its and Post-it template
- Notepad and pen

Student Supplies

- *I Wonder/I Learned* Thinksheet [See *Strategy Book 3*, page 71, or the DVD-ROM.]
- Post-its
- Clipboard and pencil

Find answers to expand thinking

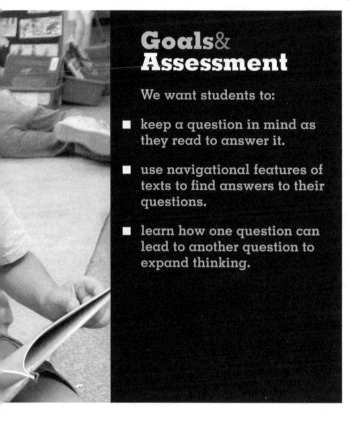

Goals & Assessment

We want students to:

- keep a question in mind as they read to answer it.

- use navigational features of texts to find answers to their questions.

- learn how one question can lead to another question to expand thinking.

Why & What

As young kids explore the wide world through nonfiction, questions become tools for research and investigation. Questions provide a window into kids' thinking—letting us peek into their developing understanding of new information. As in previous lessons, questions spark curiosity and interest, but in this lesson we build upon kids' propensity for asking questions to extend thinking and foster understanding. Kids learn practical ways to navigate informational texts, using the table of contents, key words, and other visual and text features to locate information that answers their questions.

How

Connect and Engage

- Engage kids in the text by pointing out captivating photographs and wondering about them.

- Invite kids to share out authentic questions. Record them on Post-its.

Model

- Introduce the chart and demonstrate how you keep a question in mind to answer it.

- Skim and scan the table of contents to check for information about the question.

- Locate information relating to the question.

- Ask a child to keep the meaning of an unfamiliar vocabulary word.

- Write information from the text that answers the question, using bullets.

- Have kids share out what they saw you model.

- Encourage kids to share out additional questions— questions that expand their thinking.

Guide

- Read together to look for key words from the questions and check to see if they are mentioned in the table of contents.

- Ask kids to turn and talk, prompting them to think about information that relates to the questions.

- Reiterate how a connection to background knowledge adds to understanding.

- On the chart, draw an arrow connecting learning to a new question.

Practice Independently

- Invite kids to read on their own and find answers to their questions.

- Circulate and confer with kids.

Share the Learning

- Convene the group and share out their learning.

- Wrap up by thinking about what we have learned and questions we can investigate further.

Wild Weather

Tornado

Lesson Text

Texts like *Tornado* are easy to navigate because they have clear headings and each page focuses on a specific subtopic. Some of the headings on each page are written as questions, which kids can match to their own questions as they read. A table of contents allows kids to locate specific information to find answers to their questions. Pursuing an answer to one question often leads to additional information, which builds and expands kids' knowledge. And kids find that authentic questions often have more than one answer, which nudges readers into further research.

From *Tornado* by Catherine Chambers. Copyright © 2007. Reprinted by permission of Pearson Education.

TEACHING MOVES	TEACHING LANGUAGE

Connect and Engage

Engage kids in the text by pointing out captivating photographs and wondering about them.

Take a look at this book, *Tornado*. Let's check out the photographs. On the cover is a huge tornado. I know from my background knowledge that tornadoes are powerful, dangerous storms. They have incredibly strong winds that cause a lot of damage to houses and other buildings. People's homes are destroyed. *[I page through the book, showing kids the photographs.]* When I see something amazing or learn something new, a question often pops into my head as I react to the information. How about you all? What were you wondering as you looked at these pictures? Turn and talk a minute. Then we'll share some of your questions.

OK, who is ready to share a question?

Gregory: Look at that lightning flash right next to the tornado. Do tornadoes happen during thunderstorms?

Livia: What is a tornado like?

Meredith: Do tornadoes come near the mountains where we live?

Jeremiah: What can tornadoes destroy?

Invite kids to share out authentic questions. Record them on Post-its.

Do tornadoes happen during thunderstorms?

Gregory

What is a tornado like?

Livia

Do tornadoes come near the mountains - where we live?

Meredith

These are really interesting questions. I'm going to write each of your questions on a Post-it and put your name on it. I know these are authentic questions. An *authentic question* is one we don't know the answer to and really want to find out. Today we'll be focusing on ways to answer authentic questions to expand our knowledge about a topic—in this case, tornadoes.

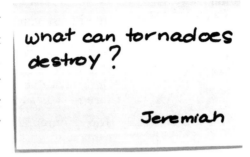

Model

Right now I'm going to show you how I keep one of these questions in my mind as I read the text and look at the pictures to try to answer it. Notice our *I Wonder/I Learned* Anchor Chart. The left-hand column, *I Wonder*, is for our questions. The right-hand column, *I Learned*, is for information that answers our questions. Let's try to answer Livia's question, "What is a tornado like?" I'll put the Post-it in the *I Wonder* column.

Introduce the chart and demonstrate how you keep a question in mind to answer it.

When we are trying to answer a question, we use nonfiction features, such as the table of contents, to help us find the information we are looking for. The table of contents lists what is in a book. It tells us the page where we can find information about many different aspects of tornadoes. I'm going to keep Livia's question in mind as I look quickly through the table of contents. I'm skimming and scanning, which means I'm reading it quickly to search for a phrase that is similar to my question, "What is a tornado like?"

Skim and scan the table of contents for information about the question.

Rather than just starting to read the book from the beginning, the table of contents helps me locate specific information—information I need to answer my question. This is pretty cool: I just noticed that some of the headings on the pages are actually written as questions.

TIP: I introduce the phrase *skimming and scanning* and also mention that it means I'm looking quickly over the text— in this case to see what's in the table of contents.

And, look, here are these questions—listed in the table of contents: *What Is a Tornado? Where Do Tornadoes Happen? Why Do Tornadoes Happen?* I think the closest question to our question, "What is a tornado like?," is *What Is a Tornado?* So let's start with that page—it says we can find information about this question on page 4.

Turn and talk about what you think you know about what a tornado is like. Then we'll see what the book says.

Now I'll start reading. As I read, notice what you see me do and say. In a minute I'll ask you to share what you see.

What Is a Tornado?

*A tornado is a moving, spinning **funnel** of wind. It swirls from a dark, towering cloud. The wind in a tornado is very strong. The tornado can suck up anything in its path.*

*The spinning wind throws everything out at the sides as it moves along. This makes a huge cloud of dust and **debris** around the tornado.*

I just want to take a minute and talk about the word *debris*. I want to make sure we all understand what it means. Debris is all the stuff—dirt, rocks, leaves and branches from trees, and many other things—that the tornado has sucked up and that becomes part of the swirling dust cloud. You can see the debris here in the photograph if you look closely.

Ask a child to keep the meaning of an unfamiliar vocabulary word.

TIP: To promote vocabulary development, we ask kids to keep words and be ready to share their new meanings with their peers.

Before we go on, who would like to keep this word, *debris*? Great, Noah! I'm going to write it down on a Post-it and write its meaning on the back. If anyone forgets what *debris* means, check with Noah. He is our word keeper for the word *debris*.

OK, now I've got information to write on the Anchor Chart—information that answers our question, "What is a tornado like?" We've got the Post-it with our question in the *I Wonder* column, and I'll write what we learned from reading in the *I Learned* column. I'm going to write what we just read, and I'm going to list the facts using bullets. I'll say, "A tornado is a strong, powerful wind that spins." I also learned that the spinning wind makes a funnel. And I learned something else—that tornadoes suck up what they touch. I'll write all this on the chart.

Write information from the text that answers the question, using bullets.

Have kids share out what they saw you model.

Now, I'm interested to hear what you noticed me doing just now to answer our question. *[I write what the kids noticed me doing in a notebook so I can use their observations to construct a* How to Read and Answer a Question *Anchor Chart later.]*

Jeanine: You read the table of contents to see if it answered your question.

Exactly, Jeanine. Good observation. I read the information in the table of contents to see which part of the text might answer my question. Then I read those pages.

Alejandra: You wrote the facts. And you put those dots.

Yes, I wrote some information and tried to not write too much. I used dots—we call them *bullets*—which help me write one fact, or one piece of information, at a time. That way I'm less likely to get confused by all the information.

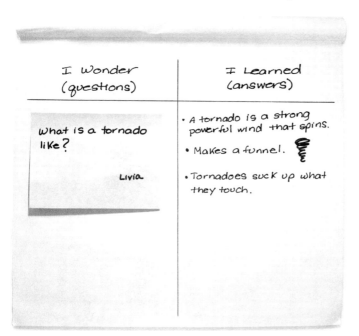

I Wonder (questions)	I Learned (answers)
What is a tornado like?	• A tornado is a strong powerful wind that spins.
	• Makes a funnel.
Livia	• Tornadoes suck up what they touch.

Javier: You used the picture. You learned from the picture.

Yes, the picture showed all the debris—dirt, dust, rocks, and broken pieces of things—swirling around in the funnel cloud. And if anyone forgets what debris is, remember to check with the official word keeper, Noah. Good observation, Javier. The picture helped us understand what the funnel cloud looks like.

Livia: I was wondering what kind of damage they do.

That's another good question. Tornadoes cause a lot of damage. Often when we learn information, we have even more questions! That's exactly what thoughtful readers do. Let's see if we can expand our thinking a bit. Let's try to find more information about tornadoes and the damage they do.

Jeremiah: That's my question, too: What can tornadoes destroy?

Thanks, Jeremiah. Let's read to try to answer both of these questions, "What kind of damage do tornadoes do?" and "What can tornadoes destroy?" We'll try to answer these questions together because they are related. Tornadoes destroy many things and cause a lot of damage.

TIP: We teach kids to bullet important information as a way to organize and list it. Teaching kids to use them replicates what we do in real life.

Encourage kids to share out additional questions— questions that expand their thinking.

Guide

Let's work together to answer the questions about the damage and destruction tornadoes cause. I'll put both questions in the *I Wonder* column. Damage and destruction are *key words*. They are important words that we will look for in the table of contents. As I read, listen for these key words. If you hear the key words *damage* and *destruction* or words that mean the same thing, stop me and we'll read that part. *[I read from the table of contents.]*

Read together to look for key words from the questions and check to see if they are mentioned in the table of contents.

What Are Tornadoes Like?

Harmful Tornadoes

Tornado Alley

Jeremiah: Stop—right there! It said *Harmful Tornadoes*—Those are tornadoes that destroy stuff.

Harmful is a key word, isn't it? It relates to tornadoes that cause a lot of damage. Let's read this part—the table of contents tells us this information is on page 14.

The winds in tornadoes travel faster than any other winds. Tornadoes usually only affect a narrow area. They destroy anything in their path.

Let's turn and talk. Here's what I want you to talk about—discuss any information you heard that relates to the damage tornadoes do and the destruction they cause. Then we'll share out. *[Kids turn and talk.]*

Jeremiah, why don't you start? I'll write the information in the *I Learned* column.

Ask kids to turn and talk, prompting them to think about information that relates to the questions.

Jeremiah: It said they destroy anything in their path. And I can see in the picture that roofs, buildings, and cars are broken.

Exactly. I'll write what you said: *Destroy houses, trees, cars—anything they hit.*

Marissa: I have a connection. I saw in the newspaper that a house was destroyed. Jeremiah said that tornadoes destroy things, and I wondered what happens to the people when a tornado comes?

Reiterate how a connection to background knowledge adds to understanding.

On the chart, draw an arrow connecting learning to a new question.

That's a thoughtful connection, Marissa. You've shared background knowledge you learned from the newspaper that helps us really understand how destructive tornadoes can be. You also asked a really important and thoughtful question about what happens to people during a tornado. We can't help but think about the terrible effects that tornadoes have on people. I'm going to write your question up here, and then I'm going to draw an arrow from the information in the *I Learned* column to your question. The arrow shows that your question came from this information. Marissa showed us that the more we learn, the more we wonder!

While I put Marissa's question on the Anchor Chart, turn and talk about what you know about tornadoes and the harm they cause. Go ahead and write any information you know about the damage tornadoes do on a Post-it. *[Kids turn and talk as I write. Then I have them share out briefly.]*

Good thinking, all of you. We're discussing serious information about tornadoes and how they affect people. You are taking information from the text and thinking more deeply about it. We started thinking about how dangerous and destructive tornadoes are, so I hope some of you will keep reading on your own now to find answers to some of these questions. And I know you will come up with other interesting questions to try to answer.

I Wonder (questions)	I Learned (answers)
What is a tornado like? Livia	• A tornado is a strong powerful wind that spins. • Makes a funnel.
What damage do tornadoes do? Livia	• Tornadoes suck up what they touch.
What can tornadoes destroy? Jeremiah	• Destroy houses, trees, cars — anything they hit!
What happens to people when a tornado comes?	

Practice Independently

If you'd like to keep going with questions about tornadoes, that's fine, and there are some books here you can use. And you are welcome to choose one of these other books on many different topics. You can use Post-its for your questions and answers, or use the *I Wonder/I Learned* Thinksheet.

[As kids read independently, I circulate around the room, conferring with them. I guide them to use text features—tables of contents, the index, and headings—to find answers to their questions.]

Invite kids to read on their own and find answers to their questions.

Circulate and confer with kids.

TIP: During a conference, I would revisit the questions several kids asked at the beginning of the lesson. Since we couldn't address all the questions during the lesson, I would confer with kids who asked them individually to guide them if they need help reading to find the answers.

Share the Learning

[Kids sit in a circle to share their questions and answers.]

Who would like to share a question they had and something they learned about it?

Convene the group and share out their learning.

> Carlos: I was thinking about what happens to people during a tornado. I think tornadoes can hurt people or maybe even kill them. I learned that if people don't get out, they could get hurt in their house if a tornado hits it.

Interesting, Carlos. You really tried to answer questions about what happens to people during a tornado. Who has some more information that might answer these questions?

> Susanna: I heard people go to the basement in a tornado; it's safer there.

> Mariah: Tornadoes are really dangerous. Just stay in the safest place you can find.

This is really important thinking. Let's continue to expand our thinking by looking for more information about this important issue you all have brought up: "How can we stay safe during a tornado?" If we are ever in a tornado, we want to have enough information to know what to do to stay safe. Let's check the table of contents in some of these books to see if we can find out how to stay safe during a tornado. I'll put this question up on the Anchor Chart. If you already have some information on tornado safety, please come and put your Post-it in the *I Learned* column. And as you read and find more information about this, please add what you've learned to the chart.

Wrap up by thinking about what we have learned and questions we can investigate further.

You've been very thoughtful about these extreme storms. You seem to understand a big idea about tornadoes. These dangerous storms can have serious effects on peoples' lives. Extreme weather is a serious topic—and now you understand so much more about it.

Did your students:

- keep a question in mind as they read to answer it?

- use navigational features of texts to find answers to their questions?

- learn how one question can lead to another question to expand thinking?

Reflect& Assess

Authentic questions are those that keep kids engaged in the search for answers. As kids navigate texts to locate information, we confer with them to assess whether they are keeping their question in mind as they read and how well they are able to determine if information they find answers their question. Kids' oral language is often more elaborate and descriptive than what they can put into writing, so we occasionally scribe their thinking. More developed readers can move into research on weather using questions as tools for investigation.

Adapt& Differentiate

This lesson was done with second graders, but here are suggestions for how to adapt and differentiate for the whole range of learners.

Emergent readers and writers share questions and answers orally and by drawing what they are learning. We scribe kids' thinking and they illustrate it (see page 57), and we encourage kids to write as much as they can to leave tracks of their thinking.

Asking and answering questions forms the foundation as kids learn to do their own research and investigations. So we guide more developed readers into the research process one question at a time. Children who are ready to use questions as tools are encouraged to write their questions, and the multiple answers they find, on a large piece of paper or a poster (see page 61). We celebrate when one question leads to another—and kids come into their own as experts on a particular topic.

Independent Practice Post-its and Responses

1 Ian was struck by some information he read—that a tornado picked up frogs and then put them down again in a new place. The book didn't say what actually happened and how the tornado sucked up the frogs, but Ian wondered how it happened. As he thought through the information, he decided a big wind had a lot to do with this amazing event. He is beginning to infer from what he reads, which I encourage as I talk with him about his thinking.

2 Lupita's question about tornadoes illustrates the important roles oral discussion and drawing play in scaffolding language and thinking. Lupita asked, "I wonder if tornadoes are big or little?" I wrote her question on the Post-It. As a child just learning English, Lupita looked through several books for photographs of tornadoes, noting that some seemed "little" and "skinny" and others much "bigger" and "fatter." After we discussed this, I asked her if she was finding information that answered her question. She replied, "Some are skinny; they don't look scary. But this one is fatter; it looks very big. It is much more scary!" Lupita then summed it up, saying, "I learned tornadoes are big and little," and drew this new information.

Questions (I wonder)	Answers (I learned)
What are torna does made of?	Tornadoes are made of 1 dirt 2 wind 3 dust

3 This child used the *Questions/Answers* Thinksheet (from Lesson 10) to organize her thinking. We encourage kids to use scaffolds as well as the strategies introduced previously.

4 Denise independently investigated the same question we asked during the lesson: What is a tornado like? She illustrated what she found out—that tornadoes are full of dust, whirl around, and have a funnel. We discussed her information about decaying tornadoes, and I clarified that tornadoes weaken and dissipate, but I made sure she understood that they do not "go back to being clouds." We celebrate that she found such interestiung information, but we correct her misconception.

Tornadoes are lighter when They First Start when it gets The ground it gets more stuff and Turns itoo darke.

lighter,

darke,

darker

5 This child used numbers in a sequence to show how a tornado becomes darker as it picks up more and more dust and debris over time. As an English Language Learner, she does her best to explain this process in writing. Her drawing helps to explain her thinking, so we encourage both.

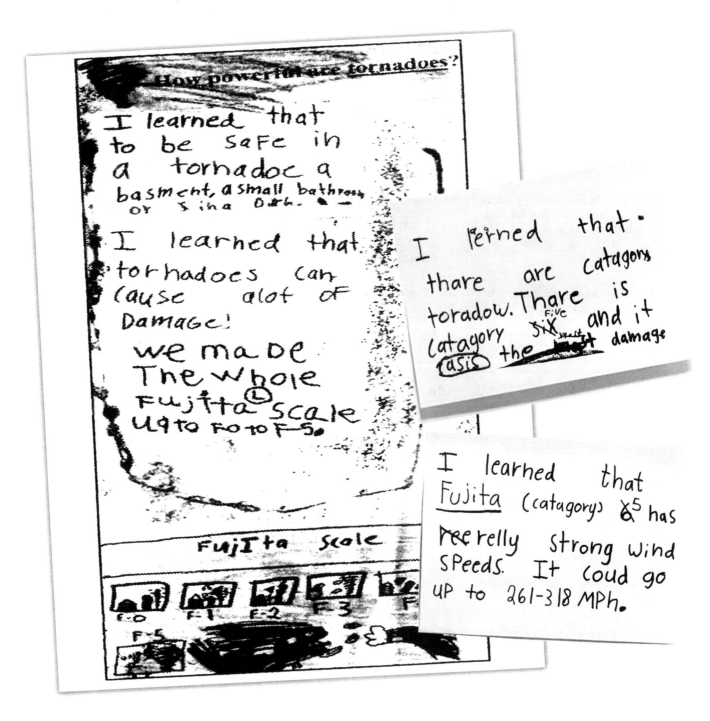

6 The two second graders who created this poster began with a question: "How powerful are tornadoes?" This question sparked others. Using the index of a weather book, they located information using the key words *tornado winds* and *wind speed*. They found a compelling graphic that described the Fujita scale—a scale designed by a meteorologist to measure tornado wind strength and speed. They wrote about this information on a poster and sketched their new learning. When kids are this engaged, they expand their learning in surprising ways, and we celebrate their independent learning.

Read with a Question in Mind

Find answers to expand thinking

TEACHING MOVES	TEACHING LANGUAGE
	Connect and Engage
Engage kids in the text by pointing out captivating photographs and wondering about them.	■ Take a look at this book. Let's check out the photographs.
	■ When I learn something new, a question often pops into my head as I react to the information. How about you? Turn and talk a minute. Then you can share some of your questions.
Invite kids to share out authentic questions. Record them on Post-its.	■ Who is ready to share a question? And another?
	■ These are really interesting questions. I'm going to write each one on a Post-it and put your name on it.
	Model
Introduce the chart and demonstrate how you keep a question in mind to answer it.	■ I'm going to show you how I keep a question in mind as I read the text and look at the pictures to try to answer it. I'm going to put the Post-its with the question on the *I Wonder/I Learned* Anchor Chart.
Skim and scan the table of contents to check for information about the question.	■ When we are trying to answer a question, we use nonfiction features, such as the table of contents, to help us find the information.
	■ I'm going to keep our question in mind as I read through the table of contents. I'm searching for a question or phrase that is similar to….
Locate information relating to the question.	■ Now I'll start reading. As I read, notice what you see me do. In a minute, I'll ask you to share what you see.
Ask a child to keep the meaning of an unfamiliar vocabulary word.	■ Thank you for being our word keeper,…. If anyone needs to be reminded of what that word means, check with….
Write information from the text that answers the question, using bullets.	■ Now I've got information to write on the Anchor Chart that answers our question. Let's put the question in the *I Wonder* column and what we learned from reading in the *I Learned* column.
Have kids share out what they saw you model.	■ I'm interested to hear what you noticed me doing just now to answer our question.
	■ Good observation. I read the information in the table of contents to see which part of the text might answer my question. I wrote some information and tried to not write too much.
Encourage kids to share out additional questions—questions that expand their thinking.	■ Who has another question? That's a good one! Often when we learn information, we have even more questions!

The Teaching Moves outline your instructional sequence and the
Teaching Language gives you an idea about what to say to your students.

TEACHING LANGUAGE	TEACHING MOVES
Guide	
■ Let's work together to answer one of your big questions. We have a couple of *key words*, important words that we can look for. We skim, or look quickly through, the table of contents for them.	Read together to look for key words from the questions and check to see if they are mentioned in the table of contents.
■ If we see these exact words, or words that mean the same thing, we'll know the information relates to our questions. Stop me and we'll read that part…OK, I will read this section aloud.	
■ Why don't you all turn and talk about any information you heard that relates to…. Then we'll share out and I'll write the information in the *I Learned* column.	Ask kids to turn and talk, prompting them to think about information that relates to the questions.
■ Who wants to share? That's a useful connection! Background knowledge like yours helps us to better understand the information.	Reiterate how a connection to background knowledge adds to understanding.
■ Good thinking. Notice that what we are learning can spark a question.	On the chart, draw an arrow connecting learning to a new question.
Practice Independently	
■ I want you to keep thinking about these questions and read on your own or find a book on a new topic and use your questions to learn more.	Invite kids to read on their own and find answers to their questions. Circulate and confer with kids.
Share the Learning	
■ Who would like to share a question they had and something they learned about it?	Convene the group and share out their learning.
■ Interesting. You really tried to answer our questions. Who has some more information that might answer our questions?	
■ This is really important thinking. You all have done a great job answering your questions, and you have added to what you know about….	Wrap up by thinking about what we have learned and questions we can investigate further.
■ Let's continue to expand our thinking by looking for more information about….	

Reflect& Assess

Did your students:

■ keep a question in mind as they read to answer it?

■ use navigational features of texts to find answers to their questions?

■ learn how one question can lead to another question to expand thinking?

Ask Questions Strategy Wrap-up:
Creating an Anchor Chart to Capture What We Learned about Asking Questions

Teaching Language

Now that we have done some lessons on asking questions when we read, listen, and view, let's take a look back at what we have learned. We can co-construct an Anchor Chart about this strategy that will serve as a visual reminder to help us remember to ask questions when we read. The *Questioning* Anchor Chart can guide us as we continue to use questioning strategies to help us understand what we read.

I'll begin by sharing something important that I do when I ask questions and then record it on the chart. For instance, I know to ask questions when I read to better understand the text. While I am jotting this down on the chart, turn to each other and talk about something you have learned about questioning that is important to consider when we read. Be sure to say it in a way that makes sense to you.

[Kids turn and talk.]

Let's share some of your thoughts.

[We want to capture kids' comments that show their understanding of the strategy as well as our lesson language to guide future teaching and learning.]

What We Learned about Questioning

We ask questions to better understand what we listen to, read, and view.

We know what it is to be curious and we are curious!

We wonder about new information.

We jot or draw our questions on Post-its or in the margins.

We understand that some questions are answered and some are not.

We change our thinking based on new information.

We ask questions when we are confused.

We read with a question in mind, so we can find an answer to it.

We answer our questions by looking at the pictures and reading the text.

We find answers to our questions by using the table of contents to locate information.

We can get our questions answered by talking to our peers.

We know that one question can lead to another and we can learn more.

Assessment Checklist for Ask Questions

Expectations for student thinking and learning

- Learn to ask questions when reading, listening, and viewing
- Learn what it is to be curious
- Wonder about new information
- Leave tracks of questions when listening, reading, or viewing
- Understand that some questions are answered and others are not
- Change thinking based on new information
- Ask questions to clarify confusion
- Keep questions in mind while reading, viewing, and listening, and search for answers
- Use navigational features, table of contents, index, etc., to answer questions and develop more questions
- Learn strategies for answering questions—read the text, look at the pictures, talk to a peer

Questions you can ask yourself to assess student understanding

- Do they ask questions before, during, and after reading, listening, and viewing?
- Do they ask questions when they meet new information?
- Do they understand what it is to be curious?
- Are they curious?
- Do they jot or draw their questions as they go?
- Do they change their thinking based on new learning?
- Do they ask questions when they are confused?
- Do they read with a question in mind?
- Do they have a variety of strategies for answering questions: reading the text, looking at the pictures and features, talking to a peer?
- Do they use the navigational features to answer and ask more questions?

Language of questioning

"I wonder..."

"I'm curious..."

"Why..."

"How come..."

"What, When, Where, Will..."

"I'm confused..."

"I don't get this..."

"I can't believe..."

"Huh?"

"My big question is..."

"I still wonder..."

"Do you know anything about..."

Annotated Rubric for Strategy Book 3:
Ask Questions

Name _____ Date _____

Oral and/or Written Evidence	Strong Evidence 3	Some Evidence 2	Little Evidence 1
Stops to ask questions when listening, reading, or viewing			
Jots and/or draws questions while listening, reading, and viewing			
Recognizes that not all questions are answered in the text			
Reads with a question in mind and tries to answer it			
Uses a variety of strategies to answer questions—looks at pictures, considers the features, reads the text, and asks a friend			

© 2008 by Stephanie Harvey and Anne Goudvis from *The Primary Comprehension Toolkit*
Portsmouth, NH: Heinemann. This page may be photocopied for classroom use only.

© 2008 by Stephanie Harvey and Anne Goudvis from *The Primary Comprehension Toolkit*
Portsmouth, NH: Heinemann. This page may be photocopied for classroom use only.

Name _____ Date _____

© 2008 by Stephanie Harvey and Anne Goudvis from *The Primary Comprehension Toolkit*
Portsmouth, NH: Heinemann. This page may be photocopied for classroom use only.

Name _____   Date _____

I Learned	**I Wonder**

© 2008 by Stephanie Harvey and Anne Goudvis from *The Primary Comprehension Toolkit*
Portsmouth, NH: Heinemann. This page may be photocopied for classroom use only.

Questions	**Answers**

© 2008 by Stephanie Harvey and Anne Goudvis from *The Primary Comprehension Toolkit*
Portsmouth, NH: Heinemann. This page may be photocopied for classroom use only.

Name _____ Date _____

I Wonder	**I Learned**

© 2008 by Stephanie Harvey and Anne Goudvis from *The Primary Comprehension Toolkit*
Portsmouth, NH: Heinemann. This page may be photocopied for classroom use only.